He Restores My Soul

HOW ANCIENT WORDS HEAL MODERN WOUNDS

BENJAMIN STRAUP

HE RESTORES MY SOUL

Copyright © 2025 by Benjamin Straup

All rights reserved. No part of this publication may be reproduced, distributed, or transmitted in any form or by any means, including photocopying, recording, or other electronic or mechanical methods, without prior written permission from the publisher, except in the case of brief quotations used in reviews, articles, sermons, or academic work.

Published by Lux Orbis Publishing, LLC

www.LuxOrbisPublishing.com

Lux Orbis — Shine Bright

Scripture Permissions

Scripture quotations marked TPT are taken from The Passion Translation®.

Copyright © 2017, 2018, 2020 by BroadStreet Publishing Group, LLC.

Used by permission. All rights reserved.

Scripture quotations marked AMP are taken from the Amplified Bible.

Scripture quotations marked NKJV, NIV, or ESV are taken from their respective translations.

All Scripture quotations are used by permission and remain the property of their respective copyright holders.

Disclaimer

This devotional reflects the author's study, pastoral insight, and interpretation of the biblical text. It is not intended to replace Scripture, but to encourage deeper encounter with Jesus Christ, our Shepherd. The content is offered for spiritual growth and personal reflection.

Cover Design and Interior Layout: Lux Orbis Publishing, LLC

For permissions or inquiries, visit www.LuxOrbisPublishing.com

Printed in the United States of America

First Edition, 2025

HE RESTORES MY SOUL

ISBN Paperback: 979-8-9941244-2-0

ISBN eBook: 979-8-9941244-0-6

ISBN Hardcover: 979-8-9941244-1-3

Library of Congress Control Number: 2025926104

To My Beloved Wife and Forever Girlfriend,

Tisha Straup,

Your steady love, wisdom, and unshakable presence have been a refuge for my soul.

You have walked beside me through valleys of refining and stood with me on mountaintops of promise.

Thank you for being the quiet pasture when I've needed rest, the still waters when my heart needed peace, and the joy-filled song that has carried me through the shadows.

As I write this dedication, we have been married for 30 years — three decades of laughter, tears, growth, and grace. You are not only my wife, but my best friend, my confidant, my covenant companion, and my forever girlfriend. Since the day we co-founded Bethesda Church NW in December of 2013, you have led with courage and compassion, grace and grit. You have stood shoulder to shoulder with me, faithfully co-laboring with Christ to build a house of faith that is presence-driven, love-rooted, and heaven-focused.

To Our Beloved Children,

Your mom and I couldn't be prouder. As I speak these words to you as your father, I know your mother's heart resonates with every one of them.

I want you to know — without question, without hesitation — how proud I am of you. Truly proud. As I write these words, my heart is overflowing with gratitude and love. I often catch myself bragging about you to anyone who will listen, but I want to be sure the ones who matter most hear it too.

My kiddos... I am proud of you.

Not just for what you accomplish, though each of you is wildly talented, compassionate, thoughtful, and full of creativity. **I am proud of you because you are ours.** Because of who you are becoming. Because of the love you carry...the love your mom and I poured into you, the love you've taken even further, the love that continues to grow in ways that amaze us.

Each of you has enriched our lives more than you will ever fully understand. We cherish your presence. **You are gifts we never stop unwrapping.**

I also want you to know this: I am a work in progress. I am still growing — learning how to love better, listen deeper, stay attuned, and be present in the ways your hearts deserve. But even in my imperfections, my desire remains steady: **to be your biggest cheerleader, to champion the dreams God planted in your hearts, and to walk beside you through every twist and turn of life.**

And because each of you carries a story, a brilliance, and a heartbeat uniquely your own, I want to speak to each of you directly:

Huntoe — Hunter

Your heart for justice, your listening ear, and your loyal spirit are like no other. You care deeply, and your loyal love for others and the world is something truly admirable. I love your laugh and your kind eyes. You've opened my eyes to the beauty of God's creation — from spiders to plants to entire bio-active ecosystems. Without you, I would have never discovered that wonder. Your passion has shaped me, son.

I am proud of the man you are! And the man you are becoming.

AaaBaaa — Ava

My baby whisperer, whose heart beats with the melody of Heaven. Your creativity, humor, and the way you cook with love instead of just ingredients — it blesses every person invited to your table. Like your name, you have always brought a song to the chorus of our lives. You are my daughter who would lay her life down for many. I love how you love others.

And I need you to know this: I'm a proud, protective dad — and I will always cherish the nights tucking in my little girl… butterfly kiss, Eskimo kiss, and regular kiss. Those memories live forever in me.

Keep singing, my little bird. Your voice carries light. **I am so proud of you!**

Logey Bear — Logan

Your resilience and quiet confidence are contagious. You have carried this strength your whole life, and when you broke your femur at age five, it only proved what was already true — you are unshakeable. Even that moment, painful and unexpected, never broke your spirit. If anything, it forged something deeper in you. It strengthened your stride — making you more confident, bold, and full of life.

I love your heart for spontaneous adventure. Your witty charm, quick mind, and fearless way of being have brought generosity and joy to everyone you meet. You see the gold in people and call it forward, often before they see it in themselves.

And that birthday fish? Yes — fish on, my fearless son. Never stop pursuing life with that wild courage I adore.

Proud of you, my son!

Min

You stepped into our family at fourteen, and from that day forward, you became a big brother to Hunter, Ava, and Logan. You are family — chosen, grafted, and deeply loved. Your heart for truth, your refusal to back down even when it costs you — these things inspire me. And I will never forget the moment you officially became American...the State Fair. You know exactly what I'm talking about. **So proud of you!**

Royalty

For 2.5 years, through the foster care system, we had the privilege of calling you daughter. You marked our family in ways we may not fully understand for years to come. You lived up to your name — Royalty. And even if our paths don't cross again, the truth remains: we all know we had the privilege of raising Royalty.

We are proud of the girl you were and the young woman you will become.

Isaiah Day

Our godson and our overcomer. We have had the honor of loving you and walking with you since you were five days old. As I write this, you are five and a half, and it takes my breath away. Your middle name declares it: This is the day the Lord has made. And we rejoice that we get to call you son.

There is a powerful call of God on your life, little warrior. I am proud of your courage already rising. And Isaiah — you will always have a home away from home with us. You're our son and family forever. **Know that I am so proud of you!**

You are each a facet of a diamond whose brilliance never dulls.

Different angles, different colors, different stories... one radiant family.

My dream — one that lives deep within me — is that when you hear your father's voice, it echoes through the hallways of your heart with winds of encouragement. That long after I am gone, you will still hear me cheering you on as you take your place in a world that desperately needs your light.

My hope and desire will always be this: to love you well, to grow with you, and to call out the greatness within you.

So I'll say it again, as loudly as these pages allow: **I am so, so, SO PROUD OF YOU!**

Always and Forever,

— Dad

To Our Amazing Parents

Michael J. & Martie Straup

George and Susie Elliot,

If we tried to capture the extravagant blessing we have received from our parents, it would become a book all its own. Your lives have been sermons that needed no pulpit — aid down for Jesus and for His most priceless treasure: people. You never merely spoke the language of faith; you embodied it. You walked in the Spirit, and you still walk there now.

Anyone who has known you has brushed shoulders with giants in the faith. To honor such a legacy is our privilege — one of the greatest gifts we carry. Dad and Mom, we LOVE YOU. We are blessed beyond what ink and paper could ever hope to measure.

Thank you for your unwavering wisdom, your steady encouragement, and for raising us on a foundation anchored in biblical truth. Each of you has served the Kingdom faithfully — as pastors, shepherds, and spiritual fathers and mothers — guiding not only our lives, but the lives of countless others with a love marked by humility, compassion, and unwavering conviction.

Because of your faithfulness, we now walk in blessings that seem ordinary but are undeniably supernatural. We feel the strength of the prayers you prayed in the dark, the seeds you sowed with tears, and the courage you modeled when no one was watching.

We do not take this inheritance lightly. We recognize the depth of your labor of love — poured out not only into us, but into your grandchildren, and into the many spiritual sons and daughters whose lives bear the fingerprints of your devotion.

We are extravagantly blessed beyond words. The legacy of your faith continues to ripple like waves across the ocean — reshaping the sands of our family line, carving new paths of grace for generations yet to come.

Thank you, from the deepest places of our hearts.

With endless love and overflowing gratitude,

— Your Children

To Bethesda Church NW

You are more than a congregation—you are a family.

You are a flock led by the Good Shepherd, a people marked by hunger for His presence and anchored in His Word. Thank you for dwelling in truth, for pursuing intimacy over image, and for becoming a house where souls are restored, prodigals come home, and weary hearts find belonging.

I am proud of you — not for what you do, but for **Whose you are.** You are a people who know their God and therefore do great exploits (Daniel 11:32). And the greatest exploit we will ever accomplish is not measured in numbers or achievements but in this one holy thing: that we live, move, and have our being by gazing at our First Love above all else — and by pointing a weary world to the beauty of our Shepherd King, Jesus.

Bethesda, you are a living testimony that when ordinary people fall in love with an extraordinary God, heaven touches earth. And I count it the honor of my life to walk this journey with you.

To Dr. Brian and Candice Simmons,

What are the chances?

You and Candice, standing at the Pool of Bethesda in Israel, opening an email from Bethesda Church NW and reading our message — and, Papa Brian, telling us you knew you were supposed to come to our newly planted church.

That miraculous moment stirred the water of our hearts and felt like divine orchestration at its finest. From that point forward, our hearts were knit together in a way only Heaven could design.

Since then, you have poured into us with relentless kindness — blessing us above and beyond, again and again. It's impossibly hard to put into words how grateful we are to know you both the way we do. Your steadfast encouragement and surrendered lives have made an indelible mark on our hearts.

Living lives surrendered — choosing the Way of Love no matter the cost — you've shown us what it truly means to follow Jesus. You've shown us what love looks like when it walks through fire and comes out radiant.

Thank you for teaching us to stay tender, to live with childlike wonder, to walk in humility, and to savor joy in every step of the journey.

Life brings curve-balls — the kind that could easily harden the heart, breed bitterness, or extinguish joy altogether. But you chose differently. You let adversity refine you, allowing the fire to deepen your faith, expand your joy, and strengthen your connection with God and people.

Your example shines like a beacon before us, lighting the path we long to follow as we grow in our own calling. We are deeply grateful for your friendship, your wisdom, and your unwavering hearts.

Thank you for not just speaking heavenly principles and biblical truths, but for embodying them—living them and being them. You are heroes to us, a spiritual father and mother, a gift we cherish with all our heart, held with tender affection and childlike awe and wonder.

— Ben & Tisha

To Paul and Sue Manwaring,

Thank you for being a steady, life-giving encouragement to us. From the very first moment we met you, we felt seen—truly seen—heard, known, and championed. You helped us put language to what had been stirring in our hearts for years, affirming who we are, the vision we carry, and the call God has entrusted to us. You have continually seen the Father and Mother within us, even when we were still discovering it ourselves.

And then there was that unforgettable moment—the 5,200-mile journey for a hug. A hug from a spiritual father. As Tisha wept in your arms, Paul, you held her with such strength and tenderness and simply said, "Everything is going to be okay." In that embrace, something settled within us—a deep reassurance that God was with us, that we were not alone, and that our tears were not a sign of weakness but of courage.

Thank you for every conversation, every laugh, and every shared tear; for beautiful meals, soul-deep talks, road trips, picnics, and the quiet warmth of simply being together. Your companionship, mentorship, and friendship have been a gift we treasure more than words can express.

You embody the heart behind Chapter 10—the table—creating space, offering welcome, bringing healing, nourishing, and honoring all who gather there. Your lives are a living expression of the Shepherd's table, a place where love is served generously and souls are restored. We are eternally grateful—not only for what you have poured into us, but for who you are. Paul and Sue, you have shaped our lives more than you know.

With all our love and honor,

— Ben and Tisha

Forewords

There are books you read.

And then there are books that read **you** — books that gently uncover places in your heart you didn't know were bruised, books that breathe when you open them, books that don't merely offer information but usher you into encounter.

This is one of those books.

Ben Straup has written something rare—something that feels ancient and modern at the same time. He Restores My Soul takes the timeless beauty of Psalm 23 and places it directly into the bloodstream of our hurried, anxious, exhausted world. These familiar words— "The Lord is my Shepherd..." —may be ancient, but the wounds they speak to are painfully contemporary. And Ben refuses to let this psalm sit on the surface. He brings it close. He presses it gently against the places where life has scraped us thin, where disappointment has left fractures, and where the world has demanded more of us than our heart could give.

Ben is uniquely qualified to write this devotional—not because of credentials, but because of character. He is a pastor in the truest, most biblical sense of the word: a shepherd who carries the weight of others with grace, a friend who listens without rushing, a leader who instinctively makes space for those who need a safe place to breathe again. I've watched him encourage the discouraged, steady the trembling, and lift the weary without ever drawing attention to himself. He embodies the very heart of Psalm 23, and that heart beats on every page of this book.

This devotional is not hurried. It is not loud. It does not force itself upon you. Like a shepherd's hand on your shoulder, it invites you—gently—into rest.

Each line of Psalm 23 becomes a doorway:

- A doorway into rest for the weary.

- A doorway into clarity for the confused.

- A doorway into healing for the wounds we've forgotten how to name.

- A doorway into hope for those who have learned to expect disappointment.

- A doorway into stillness for the soul that has forgotten how to stop.

Ben has a gift for taking a single phrase from Scripture and letting it breathe—letting it stretch its wings until it fills your mind, your imagination, your memory, and eventually your inner world. He writes devotionally, but he also writes pastorally. You can feel the shepherd's heart behind his words, pointing you consistently not toward platitudes, but toward the presence of the Shepherd-King Himself.

In these pages you will discover that "He restores my soul" is not a poetic sentiment—it is a promise.

A promise for those who feel spiritually thin.

A promise for those living in emotional drought.

A promise for those whose faith feels fragile.

A promise for those who have learned to function while secretly limping.

A promise for you.

My prayer for you as you open this devotional is simple: that you don't simply read these reflections, but that you experience them. Experience the rest that comes when the Shepherd makes you lie down. Experience the peace of quiet waters after years of internal storms. Experience the courage to walk through the valley without fear. Experience the anointing oil poured over the places where shame once shouted. Experience goodness and mercy not as concepts, but as companions.

This is living water for thirsty hearts.

This is holy balm for hidden wounds.

This is a path back to wholeness.

So take a breath.

Open your heart.

Let these ancient words speak again—with freshness, with tenderness, with power. Ben has prepared the table, but it is the Shepherd who will meet you there.

May you find, as countless saints before you have found, that the Shepherd of Psalm 23 is still leading, still healing, still restoring.

And may your soul—yes, your soul—become whole again.

— Dr. Brian Simmons

Author, The Passion Translation

For Ben & Tisha

When someone calls you a father in their life, there can easily be an initial thought of some version of hierarchy, but the truth is that the richest expression of fathers, mothers, sons, and daughters is when those relationships mature into mutual friendship. It happens in the natural family, and it should be the nature of the spiritual family as well.

This is what I experience with Ben & Tisha. I would call it enthusiastic friendship. In my opinion, it is the friendship called phileō love in Greek. It is this love of shared values that I always feel when I am with them — the love that the Apostle Peter dove into the sea to give and receive.

As I read this devotional, I can feel this love, this honour, this friendship, this desire to know, experience, give, and receive the best in every circumstance and scenario of life. It is the love that risks vulnerability, is willing to pay a price, lives to love others, and never holds back.

This is the love of the third exchange of questions and answers between Jesus and Peter in John's Gospel. From a boat Peter dove in, and after two exchanges of questions and answers, the dialogue concludes with the question, "Peter, do you have phileō love for Me?" and the reply, "Yes Lord, You know that I have phileō love for You," and it is concluded with the assignment: "Tend My sheep."

That context reminds me of this book — a love that dives in, vulnerable and passionate; a friendship forged and formed; a meal (a table) on a beach; a commissioning not in the formality of a meeting or church service, but in the open, on a beach, with wind, sun, and the smell of smoke.

In a world of so much digital relationship, Ben offers insight into going deeper — keys to life, doors to the soul, and authentic relationship.

There on that beach Peter's soul was restored, his assignment re-established, his love connection confirmed — stronger, forged through doubt and restoration.

Perhaps you will read this book on a beach, talk about it around a table, give it to someone whose soul needs restoring. But as you do, know that this devotional is written from the heart and spirit rather than the head. To that end, it needs to be allowed to permeate our spirits, perhaps even before our minds have processed it all.

So many of our relationships today do not have eyes meeting across tables — no touch, no embrace — in a world of digital friendships and unfollows. We need it so much.

"The Lord is my Shepherd" was written long before the Chief Shepherd arrived on the scene — Jesus becoming the manifestation of Psalm 23 and much, much more. And Peter, an example of a soul restored by the Chief Shepherd, invites each of us on the same journey. May this devotional guide you in the Shepherd's care to a restored soul, and into the kind of friendship that my friends Ben & Tisha live out loud.

— Paul Manwaring

Fathering People & Organisations

Preface

The Heart and Inspiration Behind My Book

Throughout my lifetime so far I've noticed a common theme. A innate desire that is central to every human being. It's a deep need to be known, loved, and cherished. A longing for the caverns of the soul to be healed, revealed, and understood in the light of perfect love. We live in a world louder, more divided, and more exhausted by soul-fatigue than ever, where voices clash and compassion can feel scarce — many are silently searching for peace that surpasses their understanding and looking for love to fill the void in all the wrong places. Since 2020, I've watched anxiety, fear, and disconnection rise like a tide, pulling countless hearts into isolation and confusion, leaving behind a deep cry for belonging. I see glimpses of hope in people—but many are unable to connect in a way that nourishes the soul beyond a moment. What I witnessed in others, I felt at times in myself.

This book wasn't written from a mountaintop of certainty—it was birthed in the valleys of my own struggles, questions, and aching places. I know what it is to feel stretched thin. I know what it is to carry battles no one sees. I know what it is to look for answers outside myself only to discover that the true answer was—and always is—a deeper knowing of my Shepherd King.

Culture says, "discover your own truth," urging us to craft identities apart from the Source of all life. But truth that shifts with emotion or opinion is like building your house on sinking sand—it cannot hold the weight of the soul. The heart longs for something solid, something eternal. Because truth is not relative—it's relational and foundational. Truth has a name. His name is Jesus.

He Restores My Soul was born out of the tension, heartache, and searching I've witnessed in the hearts of people longing to be whole—and out of the places where I, too, needed the Shepherd's voice to calm my storms. The identity crisis the world calls freedom only leads to deeper bondage—leaving beautiful souls fragmented and weary. But Psalm 23 is more than ancient poetry; it's a divine invitation to return to the life you were designed for—life with the One who made you, knows you, restores you, and leads you home.

Every line of this psalm is a doorway into rest for the weary, clarity for the confused, and healing for the wounds we've forgotten how to name. My hope is that as you turn these pages, you don't simply read them—you experience them. That they become living water to your thirsty soul.

Whether you are a lifelong believer longing to go deeper or a seeker still wondering if this love is real, I pray these ancient words awaken something within you—a sense of being fully seen, deeply known, and profoundly loved.

This is not just a book. It's the story of a Shepherd who met me in my own shadows and led me back into light. It's an invitation to journey with Him—into green pastures, beside still waters, and into the wholeness your heart was created for. Even in a fractured world, He still restores, He still heals, and He still leads us home. And there—resting in His presence—our souls can finally breathe again.

Restoration, Union, & Love,

— Benjamin Straup

Contents

Introduction	XXVII
A Sacred Invitation	XXX
1. How To Experience This Journey	1
2. The Lord Is My Shepherd; I Shall Not Want	5
3. He Maketh Me Lie Down in Green Pastures	16
4. He Leadeth Me Beside Still Waters	27
5. He Restoreth My Soul	48
6. He Leadeth Me in Paths of Righteousness for His Name's Sake	64
7. Yea Though I Walk Through the Valley of the Shadow of Death I Will Fear No Evil	80
8. Thy Rod and Thy Staff, They Comfort Me	92
9. Thou Anointest My Head with Oil; My Cup Runneth Over	107
10. Thou Preparest a Table Before Me in the Presence of Mine Enemies	118

11.	Surely Goodness and Mercy Shall Follow Me All The Days Of My Life	134
12.	And I Will Dwell in the House of the Lord Forever	146
13.	From Bummer to Glory: The Story of the Shepherd's Love	155
14.	The Fold Restores What Isolation Steals	159
15.	Final Encouragement: A Forever Invitation	167
16.	Closing Prayers and Declarations	170
My Personal Favorite Version of Psalm 23		175
About the Author		179
A Note from the Author		180

Introduction

The Inside Job

"*The Lord is my Shepherd; I shall not want...*"

These ancient words, penned by King David, have echoed through generations like a secret melody calling every weary heart home. But what if Psalm 23 is not just poetry for comfort, but a portal for transformation? What if these words are not meant merely to inspire you, but to restore you?

This is not a book about self-improvement. It's not another manual for better habits or stronger effort. This is an invitation into soul renovation—an inside job done by the Great Shepherd Himself, Jesus Christ.

It's about being washed in His Word until your mind, your emotions, your will, and even your imagination come into alignment with Truth, bringing you back to Life. It's about a supernatural upgrade—from barren to flourishing, from abandoned to adopted, from anxious to anchored, from striving to thriving.

But this upgrade is not something you achieve. It is something you receive.

It's about learning to live from a place you were always meant to thrive from—not by effort, performance, or self-improvement, but by inheritance. This is not a ladder you climb; it's a reality you awaken to.

This is the journey of your soul—from feeling wounded, overlooked, and left behind to being fully seen, deeply loved, and restored with purpose and joy.

We live in a world obsessed with the exterior—performance, possessions, appearance—but true transformation doesn't start on the outside. It starts inside. It begins when the voice of the Shepherd penetrates the cluttered, cracked caverns of the heart and calls you by name. It begins when you realize you were never meant to figure this life out alone. It begins when you see the hand of your Shepherd reaching out to lead you, feed you, heal you, and fiercely protect you.

Psalm 23 is not just a gentle lullaby for the dying. It's a victory song for the living—a map for abundant life both now and forever.

As you walk through the chapters of this book, you'll experience Hebrew words that unlock fresh revelation, like apples of gold in settings of silver. You'll encounter moments where you hear the Shepherd's voice for yourself, visualizations where old wounds are touched and new pathways in your mind and heart are formed, journal prompts where you wrestle, wonder, and awaken, and declarations and prayers that anchor your identity deeper into His love.

You'll walk valleys, feast at tables, drink from rivers, and dance across fields until you no longer recognize yourself as the struggling soul who started this journey.

Whether you have walked with Jesus for years or you're still unsure if God could ever love you, this book is for you. The Shepherd knows your name. He believes in you more than you believe in yourself. He's not looking for perfection; He's looking for your yes.

You were born for green pastures and still waters—not dry deserts and dusty dreams. You were born to hear His voice, not wander lost and lonely. You were born to feast, to flourish, to dwell in the house of love forever.

You are not too lost to be found. You are not too broken to be healed. You are not too late to be led into a life more beautiful than you can imagine.

It all starts here—with the words of Psalm 23 becoming not just verses on a page, but the melody of your restored soul.

Come.

The Shepherd is calling you. The table is set. The feast is ready.

Let the journey begin.

A Sacred Invitation
The Journey Begins Here

Pause in His Presence

Before we begin, let me name something gently—because I've felt it too.

Sometimes spiritual language, even when it is true and beautiful, can quietly stir pressure. Questions meant to invite can feel like tests. Stories of encounter can feel like comparison. Bold declarations of truth can feel like correction before connection. And at times, the voice inside filters everything through condemnation, shame, and accusation—as though we've stepped into a courtroom instead of a place of love, cross-examined instead of welcomed, measured instead of met.

I've felt that tension in my own heart—wondering if I knew enough, experienced enough, or believed well enough. If you've ever felt any of that, you don't need to resolve it before reading on. You're not behind. You're not disqualified. You're welcome here.

Right here, in this sacred pause, I want to ask you a question—not to judge you, test you, or put you on trial, but to awaken something already stirring within you.

Do you know Him?

Not just knowing about Him—not the stories, the facts, or the religion—but knowing Him personally and relationally. For some, that knowing comes through unmistakable moments of encounter. For others, it grows slowly—through trust, questions, and even disappointment. And for many, it begins as a quiet longing that has not yet found language. Often, it is all of these woven together in the journey of a single life.

All of it belongs here, with Jesus—our Shepherd.

He sees you—your pain and your victories, your sorrows and your beauty, the gut-wrenching moments and the glorious ones. He never leaves or forsakes you. He promises to be with you always, even to the end. He is the Shepherd of sorrow and triumph in the same breath—the Restorer of dignity, the Silencer of accusation, the One who removes sin across your entire timeline. Not reluctantly, but because you are irresistibly priceless to Him.

This is the gospel—the good news—not a doctrine to memorize, but a love story to encounter. It is the story of the God who refused to live without you, the God who crossed eternity to rescue you, the God who calls you by name because He never stopped thinking about you.

It is a reality so breathtaking it almost feels too good to be true. It is peace that quiets the noise in your mind, and a joy that does not deny sorrow but can rise alongside it. Not a forced smile. Not a demand to be okay. But the quiet strength of knowing you are not alone—even in heartbreak.

Here—at last—shame begins to lift. Emptiness loosens its grip.

This is a love that never asks for perfection, for He knows all about you, inside and out. A love that opens its arms and says, Come home as you are...and let My love rewrite your story.

At the very center of this love—shimmering like the diamond heart of Heaven—is forgiveness. Forgiveness not earned or bargained for. Forgiveness not based on how many times you've failed. Forgiveness that keeps no record and resurrects no past.

He is the kind of Forgiver who runs toward you while you're still far off, who lifts your chin when you cannot look up, who kisses the scars the world left on you and whispers, "It's already taken care of." Forgiveness is not merely something Jesus gives—it is who He is.

And when you encounter Him, you may wonder how you ever lived without Him, only to realize, in the same breath, that He was always there.

He is the moment your record is wiped clean. The moment you discover your name has always been written on His heart. The moment Heaven's love story becomes your story.

So what is this Good News?

It is not an idea. It is not a philosophy. He is a Person. His name is Jesus.

He is not a myth or a distant deity. He is the Good Shepherd who left everything to find you. Even now, He stands at the door of your heart and knocks. If you feel unsure, take one small step closer anyway. He never forces His way in.

Jesus is not the reflection of those who hurt or disappointed you. He is not the betrayal you endured, the religion that wounded you, or the person who used God's name to steal your innocence, silence your voice, or crush your dreams. He is love—fierce, patient, unwavering. He is forgiveness embodied.

So I invite you to ask yourself:

If this love—this grace, this forgiveness—is more beautiful than I ever imagined…what is holding me back from opening the door?

Take a moment. Breathe slowly. See yourself standing before the door of your heart. With each step forward, the grip of guilt, fear, and heaviness loosens. Your hand touches the handle, and warmth flows through you—the warmth of a love that has been waiting patiently for this very moment. The cares of the world and the pain of your past begin to melt away.

You feel it—the Someone you were always born for.

You open the door.

And there He is.

Eyes like fire and gentleness all at once. A gaze that does not flinch at your past or recoil from your wounds. A presence that does not merely tolerate you, but delights in you. With one look, shame dissolves. Regret loosens its hold.

For the first time, you feel home—seen, known, forgiven.

And now, as your heart stirs, whisper these words—not as a script, but as the honest cry of your soul:

Jesus, thank You for saving me. Thank You for forgiving me—fully, freely, forever. Thank You for taking my sin—past, present, and future.

Thank You for dying and rising so I could live. I receive Your love and Your forgiveness now. Enter every part of me and make me whole. Heal what is broken. Renew my spirit. Live in me and shape me into who I was always meant to be. I surrender. I trust You. Amen.

Now…pause.

Let this moment breathe. Do not rush on. Let His presence soak into the deepest places of your soul.

Chapter 1
How To Experience This Journey

This is not just a book to read—it's a life to step into.

If you allow it, these words will become a doorway: a doorway into still waters, green pastures, fierce love, and the kind of soulful restoration you were made for. To get the most out of this journey, begin by finding a quiet space. Let distractions fall away so you can hear the Shepherd's voice without hurry or pressure.

Keep a journal nearby. Along the way, you'll be invited to write, wonder, and respond as truth meets your real life. Pause often and picture what you're reading. Each chapter includes **Soul Activations**—sacred spaces to visualize the living Word washing over you and forming new pathways of healing and hope.

Pray and expect. Even a simple prayer— *"Shepherd, here I am. Lead me."*—can open the floodgates of Heaven. And come as you are. You don't have to clean yourself up to draw near. Your broken places are safe here. Your questions are welcome. Your soul is deeply desired.

This journey is not about striving harder; it's about being led—being made whole by Someone stronger, gentler, and more faithful than you've ever known. And know this: you're not reading alone. The Shepherd Himself is near.

The Journey Within Each Chapter

Each chapter is designed to draw you deeper—from revelation to response, from hearing truth to living it. As you move through the book, you'll encounter three invitations that build upon one another, guiding your soul gently and intentionally.

First, you'll step into **Soul Activations**—moments to slow down, breathe, and let the living Word wash over you. These are invitations to picture yourself in the story, to listen for the Shepherd's voice, and to let Him speak directly to your heart. This is where truth begins to move from head knowledge to heart reality.

From there, you'll enter **Journal Prompts**—sacred pauses that invite honest dialogue with your soul. As you write, allow what's stirring within you to unfold naturally. Don't rush. Sometimes healing comes through words, sometimes through tears, and often through the quiet realization that you are seen, known, and loved right where you are.

There is also a divine and scientific reason these prompts matter. God designed your mind with something called the **Reticular Activating System**—the part of your brain that acts like a gatekeeper. It notices what you focus on, scans for what matters to you, and amplifies whatever questions you ask. When you ask fear-filled questions, your mind looks for fear. When you ask faith-filled questions, your mind begins to look for your Great Shepherd, the Author and Finisher of your faith (Hebrews 12:2).

This is why Jesus so often responded with questions. He wasn't testing people; He was awakening them. Journal prompts guide your attention toward truth, hope, and healing rather than repeating old patterns. As you write, wonder, and ask the right questions, you're opening your mind to recognize what God is already revealing. You're teaching your soul to discern His voice, His goodness, and His nearness in places where you once only saw confusion or pain.

Finally, you'll encounter **Now Declarations**—spoken alignments with Heaven's truth. These declarations are not wishful thinking; they are anchors of identity, calling forth who you already are and what already belongs to you because the Lord is your Shepherd. Speaking them aloud engages your heart, soul, and body, aligning your whole being with Heaven's reality.

Activating the "Now"

Life often teaches us to place our emotions in the hands of our experiences. Disappointment, hurt, or neglect can cause those emotions to wrap tightly around certain moments, convincing us they define what is true. But what if that same passion could be redirected toward a higher reality?

The declarations throughout this book are not denials of your past; they are invitations into your present. They awaken your heart to what is already true in Christ and help your soul attach powerful, life-giving emotion to Heaven's words over you. At first, speaking them may feel unfamiliar—even untrue—especially if your current reality seems to argue otherwise. That's okay. Speak them anyway. Speak them often. Speak them boldly.

As you do, imagine the same energy once poured into fear, shame, or rejection being poured into peace, abundance, and joy. These are not just declarations; they are the song your Shepherd is already singing over you. Now, it's your turn to join in.

Navigating the Scriptures

Throughout this book, you'll notice Scripture woven naturally into each chapter. These references are not meant to overwhelm but to provide a firm foundation, grounding each truth in God's promises. As you read, allow the message to flow without stopping at every verse. Once you've completed the Soul Activations, Journal Prompts, and Now Declarations, return to the Scriptures. Open your Bible. Meditate on them. Speak them aloud. Let them seal what the Shepherd has begun to reveal.

God's Word is alive and active (Hebrews 4:12) and will not return void (Isaiah 55:11). My prayer is that as you engage with His Word, your soul will be established in truth, your identity deeply rooted, and your life infused with His promises.

This book is not meant to be read—**it's meant to be experienced**. It's a journey of belonging, believing, and becoming, one that will carry you beyond words on a page into encounter with the Living Word Himself.

Chapter 2

The Lord Is My Shepherd; I Shall Not Want

Psalm 23:1

Ever Present and Lacking Nothing

Before we can journey anywhere else, we must stop and let this breathtaking reality wash over us like living water. The Lord—Yahweh (Exodus 3:14), the Almighty, the Creator of galaxies, the One who spoke the cosmos into being—is not distant from you.

He is your Shepherd (John 10:11).

Not a ruler barking commands from a throne. Not a cold commander tallying your failures. Not a rescuer who swoops in from afar. He is near (Psalm 145:18). He is tender (Isaiah 40:11). He is attentive (1 Peter 5:7). He is a friend who sticks closer than a brother (Proverbs 18:24). He is wild with love over you (Zephaniah 3:17). And—wonder of wonders—He is also your Bridegroom King.

You are His beloved, the one He calls beautiful, flawless, and always worth pursuing (Song of Songs 4:7; 6:4–5 TPT). His gaze is locked on you. His voice sings with delight over you. His heart burns with covenant love that refuses to let you go.

You were fashioned to lean into His heartbeat—to let the Shepherd's voice guide you through every valley and onto every mountaintop. He doesn't just guide your steps; He shepherds your heart until it rests fully in His embrace and knows beyond all doubt, *"I am my Beloved's, and my Beloved is mine"* (Song of Songs 6:3 TPT).

The Hebrew Meaning of Shepherd

The Hebrew word for shepherd is **Ra'ah**—'to feed, to tend, to care for, to befriend' (Genesis 48:15). It paints the picture of One who never takes His eyes off His sheep, whose very life is wrapped up in their protection, nourishment, and flourishing (Ezekiel 34:11–12).

This Shepherd is not passive or permissive. He is actively, relentlessly, lovingly committed to you (Isaiah 41:10). He is not only a shepherd by function; He is a shepherd by nature.

The Nature of the Shepherd's Heart

To understand the Shepherd is to understand love that restores identity and reshapes the way we see everything—God, ourselves, and others. His love is not fragile or fleeting. It is the love described in 1 Corinthians 13:4–8: patient, kind, unselfish, enduring, and almost too good to be true.

It is a love that bears all things, believes all things, hopes all things, and endures all things—even when we stumble, wander, or forget who we are (Romans 8:38–39). His love never fails (1 Corinthians 13:8).

When Moses cried, *"Show me Your glory,"* God revealed what His glory truly is—the fullness of His nature and character: *"The LORD, the LORD God, compassionate and gracious, slow to anger, and abounding in lovingkindness and truth..."* (Exodus 34:6–7).

The glory of the Shepherd is His goodness. His compassion is not reluctant; it overflows. His mercy is not rationed; it abounds. His patience is not strained—it is anchored in everlasting love (Jeremiah 31:3).

If you could peer into His heart, you would see it bursting with the fruit of the Spirit—love, joy, peace, patience, kindness, goodness, faithfulness, gentleness, and self-control (Galatians 5:22–23). Every step He takes toward you is saturated with these fruits (John 15:9). Every word He speaks is soaked in this character (John 1:14).

He is not harsh with you (Isaiah 42:3). He is not frustrated with you (Psalm 103:13–14). He is not waiting for you to perform better before calling you His own (Romans 5:8). He has already called you friend (John 15:15). You are already His (John 10:28). You are already loved (1 John 4:19).

The Lion-Hearted Shepherd

But make no mistake—His tenderness is not weakness. The heart that cradles lambs is the heart of a Lion (Revelation 5:5). It took the heart of a Lion to become the Lamb slain before the foundation of the world (Revelation 13:8).

His love is fierce, willing to battle wolves, cross canyons, and descend into the darkest valleys to rescue you (Luke 15:4–6). He stands over you with authority, shielding you from every enemy of your soul (Psalm 91:4). The Lion's heart beats behind the Shepherd's hands (Exodus 15:3).

This is no fragile affection. It is covenantal ferocity—protective, strong, and unyielding (Psalm 89:34; Deuteronomy 31:6). He is gentle enough to restore your soul (Isaiah 40:11) and mighty enough to destroy your enemies (Isaiah 54:17).

The Shepherd who carries you also conquers for you.

You are His lamb—safe in His arms, protected by His fierce love. The Lamb saved you. The Lion guards you. The Shepherd carries you. And you—His lamb—are forever safe.

Ḥāsēr: The Illusion of Lack

The second half of this verse— *"I shall not want"*—is equally transformative. In Hebrew, it is **lo ḥāsēr**: *I will not lack*. **Ḥāsēr** means 'to be in need, deficient, diminished, or incomplete.'

But in covenant with Yahweh Ra'ah, the declaration flips. *I am complete. I am full. I am whole.*

Because the Shepherd is mine, lack is an illusion.

You may not have everything the world says you should want, but you are not lacking. You are not missing a vital piece. You are not behind. The lie of lack is simply the soul forgetting its Shepherd. When you return to Him, you return home to truth: *You lack nothing because He is everything.*

"All that I have is already yours." (Luke 15:31)

Identity Restored

The greatest place people feel lack is not in possessions; it is in identity. The lie whispers, *"I am not enough...because I don't have enough"* (Luke 12:15). And it goes deeper still: *I am what happened to me. I am the mistake I made. I am the label they gave me.*

For many, these lies masquerade as freedom—rewriting identity, reshaping the body, following feelings in hopes the ache will disappear. But these promises are hollow. They offer moments of relief without lasting peace. They cannot anchor the soul.

The Shepherd King kneels beside the weary, the ashamed, and the striving and says, *"I see you. I know the story behind your tears. I'm not here to condemn you—I'm here to heal you."* *"The LORD is close to the brokenhearted..."* (Psalm 34:18).

He sees past your masks and your striving. He sees beyond your past and even beyond what you believe about yourself (1 Samuel 16:7). He sees the real you—the one He formed in love (Jeremiah 1:5), the one He calls by name (Isaiah 43:1), the one He paid everything to redeem (1 Peter 1:18–19).

This isn't about shame; it's about freedom. Freedom that lifts your head, steadies your heart, and calls you into the truest version of you. *"If the Son sets you free, you will be free indeed"* (John 8:36).

You are not lacking—you are already loved. Always have been. Always will be.

Gaze So You Can Graze

You become like what you behold (Hebrews 12:2). When your identity is consumed by the lie of lack, you will always feel less-than. But when your gaze is fixed on the Shepherd, you begin to graze in the right pasture—a pasture overflowing with His goodness (Psalm 16:6; 34:8).

In His presence, false identities dissolve. The pressure to prove fades. The truth of who you are is settled once and for all. You are already complete in Him (Colossians 2:10). Perhaps the only thing left is to see yourself the way He sees you.

Gaze at your Shepherd King, and graze in the abundance of His presence.

Jesus doesn't erase your identity—He redeems it. He shatters chains of conformity masquerading as freedom and speaks the truth that has always been yours: You are His masterpiece (Ephesians 2:10). When He restores you, He restores the whole you—body, soul, and spirit—until even secret tears give way to joy no one can take (John 16:22).

Soul Activation

Gaze and Graze

Find a still moment and let your breathing settle. Allow the noise around you to fade as you picture the Shepherd stepping toward you—calm, sure, and full of unwavering love. His presence quiets the anxious places inside you.

Look into His eyes. They hold galaxies of compassion, oceans of understanding, and a love that sees straight through your defenses without wounding you. He knows where you've been. He knows what you've carried. He knows the story behind every tear you've swallowed—and He is not ashamed of you. Not one bit.

He places His hand over your heart, not to judge, but to steady. In that touch is the truth your soul longs for: *You are Mine. You are loved. You lack nothing.*

Feel the weight you've carried begin to loosen. Let His nearness silence every lie of lack, every pressure to perform, every false identity that tried to cling to you. Breathe in His peace. Breathe out the striving. Let the Shepherd lead your soul into rest—a rest that restores, reminds, and anchors you in His love.

Stay here as long as your heart needs. Let Him shepherd you.

Journal Prompts

1. Where have I been living from the illusion of lack? What fear, story, or assumption keeps whispering *"not enough"* over my life? (Psalm 23:1; Luke 15:31)

2. Which part of the Shepherd's nature is hardest for me to believe is true for me — His nearness, tenderness, delight, or identity over me — and why? (Psalm 145:18; Zephaniah 3:17; 1 John 4:16)

3. Where have I confused performance with worth, tying who I am to what I do instead of to whose I am? (Ephesians 2:8–10)

4. What identity labels or internal narratives is Jesus inviting me to surrender at the Shepherd's feet so I can live from what He has always spoken over me? *"I am what happened to me..." "I am a mistake..." "I am too much..." "I am not enough...".* (Isaiah 43:1; Psalm 34:18; John 8:36)

5. Where have I tried to rewrite my own identity apart from the One who made me, and how has that pursuit promised freedom but produced exhaustion? (Psalm 139:13–14; Proverbs 14:12)

6. How does knowing my Shepherd says, *"All that I have is already yours,"* **invite my perspective to align with the truth that I am not lacking in Him?** (Luke 15:31; Colossians 2:10)

7. Today, where do I sense the Shepherd calling me into deeper trust, surrender, or belonging — and what is one simple *"yes"* **I can give Him in response?** (Luke 1:38)

Now Declaration

I Am Who He Says I Am

I am shepherded by Yahweh — my Defender and Friend.

I am completely known, deeply loved, and fully held (Psalm 139:1–4).

I am not lacking — I am complete in Christ (Colossians 2:10).

I am free from the illusion of lack and rooted in divine abundance.

I am not striving to become — I am resting in who I already am in Him.

I am seen, safe, and sustained by the eyes that never leave me (2 Chronicles 16:9).

I am grazing in peace-full-joy because my gaze is set on the Good Shepherd (Psalm 34:8).

I am attuned to the voice of love, not fear — the voice of my Shepherd (John 10:27).

I am not forgotten — I am called by name and carried in covenant (Isaiah 43:1).

I am His masterpiece — a one-of-a-kind, fearfully and wonderfully made (Ephesians 2:10; Psalm 139:14).

I am no longer defined by what happened to me — I am defined by what He did for me.

I am free from the labels of man and marked by the love of God.

I am living from acceptance, not working for it.

I am loved without condition, restored without limit, and secured without fear.

Final Reflection

My Shepherd

Two words that restore everything — "My Shepherd."

Not distant. Not borrowed.

Personal. Present. Yours.

The Creator of galaxies is attuned to your heart — near, tender, and true.

In His gaze, striving ceases and belonging begins.

You are no longer chasing identity or searching for home — you already are, and always will be, His.

His love is extravagant, and His care completely includes you.

The Lord is my Shepherd, I shall not want.

Chapter 3

He Maketh Me Lie Down in Green Pastures

Psalm 23:2a

The Beauty of Being Made to Rest

"*He makes me lie down...*" (Psalm 23:2)

The beauty of the word make is not control—it is creation. Your Shepherd is also your Maker (Psalm 100:3), and when He makes you lie down, He isn't forcing you; He is forming something in you that only He can.

When your thoughts spiral with anxiety and your emotions tremble under the weight of depression, when no escape seems possible and false comforts only deepen the ache, He comes. Not with shame. Not with impatience. But with mercy—and knowing. He knows you've tried everything. He knows you've carried more than anyone realizes. And just when you feel like you can't hold it together anymore, He holds you.

He makes you lie down—not as punishment, but as rescue. Not to control you, but to comfort you. Not to silence you, but to still the noise that has been stealing your breath. You could never make this happen on your own. But He can, and He does.

"It is the LORD who goes before you. He will be with you; He will never leave you nor forsake you. Do not fear or be dismayed." — Deuteronomy 31:8

When You're Too Worn Out to Keep Going

Let's be honest—there are moments when you've fought to stay afloat, smiled while your heart was breaking, and pushed through even as your soul ran empty. But the Shepherd sees it all. He knows the trauma, the betrayal, the disappointment. He knows the nights you wept when no one was watching, and the moments you questioned whether peace was even real.

And instead of demanding that you try harder, He comes closer.

He kneels beside your trembling soul, brushes the dust from your face, and whispers, *"Come to Me, all who are weary and burdened, and I will give you rest."* — Matthew 11:28

With fierce compassion, He lays His hand on your chest, and the spinning begins to slow. The fear loosens. The weight starts to lift. He makes you lie down not because you're defeated, but because you are deeply loved.

He's not the Shepherd who waits for you to figure it out. He is the One who sits in the valley with you and says, *"You don't have to carry this anymore. I've already carried you."* — Isaiah 46:4

And when you finally collapse into His presence—when you stop trying to hold everything together and let yourself be held—you realize the mystery has been true all along: *"In your weakness, He is strong."* — 2 Corinthians 12:9

This is restoration your soul forgot was even possible.

The Shepherd Intervenes: The Fullness of Salvation

The Hebrew doesn't say, *"He suggests I lie down."* It says, *"He makes me."* Like a shepherd who gently but firmly causes his sheep to rest because without rest they collapse, and without stillness they will die chasing what they were never meant to pursue.

This isn't about passivity. It's about salvation.

The Greek word **Sōzō (σῴζω)** means far more than *"saved from hell."* It speaks of wholeness and rescue in every dimension: deliverance from danger (Psalm 91:3), healing in body, mind, and soul (Isaiah 53:5), preservation from harm (2 Timothy 4:18), and restoration to your original design (Psalm 23:3). It is wholeness—lacking nothing (James 1:4).

He doesn't just pull you back from the edge. He makes you whole again.

"The LORD is my strength and my song; He has become my salvation." — Exodus 15:2

The Resistance to Rest

One of the deepest battles of the human soul is resistance to rest—yet the first thing the Shepherd does after leading you is make you lie down.

We tell ourselves, *I have to earn it. I don't deserve it yet. Rest comes after I fix everything. If I stop, I'll fall behind. God is more pleased with my work than with my stillness. If I'm not doing something, I'm not valuable.*

But green pastures are not a reward for finishing the journey; they are the starting point of it.

Our Shepherd knows sheep won't lie down unless they feel safe, full, and secure. So He doesn't simply invite us to rest—He makes us. Not as a tyrant, but as a tender Guardian who knows our strength is renewed only in stillness.

To lie down in green pastures is to trust His provision enough to stop striving. It is to believe the world will keep spinning without your constant effort. It is to embrace that His pleasure is not in your pace, but in your presence with Him.

The green pasture is more than a soft place to land. It is a sacred space to be restored, the Shepherd's way of saying: you don't have to keep proving yourself. You don't have to scan the horizon for danger—I am watching for you. You don't have to search for your next meal—I've already prepared it.

You can stop. You can breathe. You can be.

"For anyone who enters God's rest also rests from their works, just as God did from His." — Hebrews 4:10

The Maker Knows How You're Made

He makes you lie down not just because He's Shepherd, but because He's Maker. You weren't created to live in overdrive. You were never designed to be powered by pressure, fear, or performance. Your frame was knit together by hands of love (Psalm 139:13), and the One who made you knows exactly how to restore you.

"We are His workmanship..." — Ephesians 2:10

The Greek word for workmanship is **poiēma**—'His poem, His artwork, His carefully crafted masterpiece.' He doesn't just understand your wiring; He designed it. He doesn't merely tolerate your need for rest; He celebrates it.

Because rest isn't weakness. It's alignment.

Your Creator formed your soul to flourish through rhythm—to inhale His presence and exhale the strain, to pause, to be, to let Him hold what you were never meant to carry. He makes all things new, and you are no exception (Revelation 21:5).

You are not a machine to be fixed. You are a masterpiece being restored. And sometimes the most holy thing He can do is lay you down—not to stop you, but to start something deeper in you than you ever imagined.

Green Pastures: A Place of Overflow

The Hebrew word for pastures is **Naveh**—'a beautiful dwelling place, a habitation of rest.' It isn't a dusty patch of dirt; it is a vibrant, soul-rich space overflowing with provision (Philippians 4:19), belonging

(Psalm 68:6), safety (Proverbs 18:10), beauty (Song of Songs 2:10–13), abundance (Psalm 36:8), and nourishment (Isaiah 55:1–2).

"He will be standing firm like a flourishing tree planted by God's design, deeply rooted by the brooks of bliss, bearing fruit in every season of life. He is never dry, never fainting, ever blessed, ever prosperous." — Psalms 1:3 (TPT)

This is where He lays you down—not because you've earned it, but because He refuses to let you live in survival mode. Here, even now, He is restoring your soul.

Soul Paradigm Shift: Rest Is a Gift, Not a Reward

If you believe you have to earn rest, you'll never truly enter it. You'll always chase, strive, and perform—never realizing you're running from the very thing you most desperately need.

But when you believe rest is a gift from your Shepherd, you can finally let go.

"There remains, then, a Sabbath-rest for the people of God… Let us, therefore, make every effort to enter that rest." — Hebrews 4:9–11

Rest is not laziness; it is obedience (Matthew 11:28). Rest is not weakness; it is warfare (Hebrews 4:12). Rest is not failure; it is faith (Psalm 46:10). Rest is not avoidance; it is alignment (Isaiah 30:15). Rest is not passivity; it is positioning (Exodus 14:14).

Rest is the war cry of a child who knows they are safe in the Father's arms.

Soul Activation

Let Him

Find a quiet place and breathe deeply.

Picture yourself in a wide-open field—the grass soft, the wind gentle, the air clean.

The Shepherd comes to you and looks into your eyes with the kind of love that breaks every wall and speaks directly to the weariness in your soul: *"Lie down, beloved. You don't have to fight anymore."*

And for the first time in a long time, you let yourself be held. You let go. You rest. You are being remade by mercy.

Stay here as long as you need.

Journal Prompts

1. Where have I been resisting the Shepherd's invitation to rest — and what fear or belief is keeping me from lying down? (Matthew 11:28; Isaiah 30:15)

2. What would shift in my life if I trusted Him enough to stop striving and truly lie down in the green pastures He provides? (Psalm 23:2; Hebrews 4:10)

3. What belief do I need to release in order to embrace rest as a gift, not a reward I must earn? (Hebrews 4:9–11)

4. Where have I been carrying burdens He has already promised to hold — and what does laying them down look like today? (1 Peter 5:7; Isaiah 46:4)

5. How does knowing I am His workmanship — His poiēma — reshape the way I view my limits, my need for rest, and my worth? (Ephesians 2:10; Psalm 139:13–14)

6. What happens in my soul when I let myself be held instead of holding everything together? (2 Corinthians 12:9; Deuteronomy 31:8)

7. Where is the Shepherd forming something in me through rest that I could never produce through striving? (Psalm 23:3; Philippians 1:6)

Now Declaration

The Gift of Rest

I am held by my Shepherd, who makes me lie down in love — not control. (Psalm 23:2)

I am safe to rest. I am not forgotten or failing — I am cherished and remembered. (Deuteronomy 31:8)

I am not earning rest — I am receiving it as a gift. My value is not in what I do, but in who I am to Him. (Matthew 11:28)

I am restored in green pastures — surrounded by beauty, nourished by peace, and rooted in love. (Psalm 1:3; Isaiah 55:2)

I am no longer driven by pressure — I am drawn by grace. Stillness is my strength. (Isaiah 30:15)

I am made whole — spirit, soul, and body — by the One who knows me better than I know myself. (1 Thessalonians 5:23; Psalm 147:3)

I am led to quiet places where my soul can breathe again. (Jeremiah 31:25; Psalm 23:3)

I am not a burden to my Shepherd — I am His delight. He comes close with compassion, not demands. (Isaiah 46:4)

I am healed by rest, strengthened by surrender, and renewed by stillness. (2 Corinthians 12:9; Hebrews 4:10)

I am His workmanship — handcrafted by Love, created for rest, beauty, and joy. (Ephesians 2:10)

I am who He says I am — completely loved, fully held, and finally at rest. (Galatians 4:7; Hebrews 4:11)

Final Reflection

The Gift of Being Made to Rest

Sometimes love looks like being stopped.

He makes you lie down — not to limit you, but to love you back to life.

The Shepherd who formed you knows when your soul can no longer run on empty.

He is aware of every breath, every burden, every unspoken need.

Where striving ends, healing begins and in His presence, rest is not earned — it's received.

You are not falling behind; you are being restored.

This is not the end of your strength — it's the beginning of trusting your Maker, of knowing that in your weakness the Shepherd is strong (Joel 3:10).

He makes me lie down in green pastures.

Chapter 4
He Leadeth Me Beside Still Waters
Psalm 23:2b

The Stillness of the Shepherd

We live in a world that moves too fast. Noise, urgency, and distraction have become normal, but your soul was never designed to live frantic. *"Come back to me! By returning and resting in Me you will be saved. In quietness and trust you will be made strong"* (Isaiah 30:15 TPT).

Your soul was made for a disposition of stillness. *"Be still and know that I am God"* (Psalm 46:10)—or you could say, rest in a deep knowing trust of your Shepherd.

Stillness is not passivity; it is power. It is where clarity is born (Psalm 62:1), restoration takes root (Isaiah 58:11), and creativity awakens as identity is affirmed (Psalm 46:10). The Great Shepherd knows this, which is why He doesn't merely invite you to stillness—He leads you there. *"Are you weary, carrying a heavy burden? Come to me. I will refresh your life, for I am your oasis"* (Matthew 11:28–29 TPT).

In stillness, you remember who He is (Psalm 46:10). And in that remembering, you begin to remember who you are (Colossians 3:3).

Momentum Without Stillness: The Trap of Busyness

Fear often provides a counterfeit fuel. It doesn't shout—it whispers. Hurry, or something bad will happen. It drives you not from vision, but from dread. "For God will never give you the spirit of fear, but the Holy Spirit who gives you mighty power, love, and self-control." (2 Timothy 1:7 TPT).

You may look driven on the outside, but inside your compass points to survival, not security. You're achieving, but you're miserable. That's why stillness is not the loss of momentum—it is your true momentum. Stillness doesn't stop purpose; it sanctifies it. It births sustainable movement that flows from peace instead of panic, from love instead of lack.

Fear's Counterfeit Fuel: 15 Unhealthy Motivators

Any one of these can quietly run your life. Most people carry several at once—without ever naming them. But naming them is where freedom begins. The question isn't whether fear has spoken. It's whether you've been listening.

1. Fear of Falling Behind: "I have to keep going or I'll fall behind." → Comparison replaces contentment.

2. Fear of Being Seen as Lazy: "If I slow down, I'll look lazy." → Turns rest into guilt.

3. Fear of Collapse: "If I rest, everything will fall apart." → You hold life together in your strength.

4. Fear of Facing Yourself: "If I stop, I'll have to face what's inside." → Avoids healing and truth.

5. Fear of Disappointing Others: "If I say no, they'll leave." → People-pleasing erodes boundaries.

6. Fear of Never Being Enough: "If I don't achieve more, I'm not enough." → Achievement becomes identity.

7. Fear of Losing Control: "If I let go, life will spin out." → Over-management and mistrust.

8. FOMO: "If I don't say yes, I'll miss my chance." → Frantic striving, poor priorities.

9. Fear of Rejection: "If I don't perform, I won't be loved." → Love becomes earned, not received.

10. Fear of Irrelevance: "If I'm not visible, I'll be forgotten." → Image management over authenticity.

11. Fear of Failure: "If it's not perfect, I lose everything." → Perfectionism, procrastination, paralysis.

12. Fear of Punishment: "If I mess up, I'm shamed." → Legalism and hyper-vigilance.

13. Fear of Scarcity: "If I don't grab now, there won't be enough." → Hoarding, competitiveness, striving.

14. Fear of Exposure: "If I slow down, they'll see my weaknesses." → Insecurity masked by activity.

15. Fear of Letting Others Down: "If I don't hold it all, they'll suffer." → False savior-complex and pressure.

This kind of momentum doesn't strengthen you—it slowly breaks you, breeding dread, deepening anxiety, and using shame as fuel as it whispers, "Hurry, or something bad will happen," driving you not from vision but from the fear of punishment.

"Love never brings fear, for fear is always related to punishment. But love's perfection drives the fear of punishment far from our hearts..." – 1 John 4:18 TPT

You may look driven on the outside, but inside your compass points to survival rather than security—you're achieving, yet you're miserable, which is why stillness is not the loss of momentum but the recovery of your true momentum; stillness does not stop purpose, it sanctifies it, birthing sustainable movement that flows from peace instead of panic and from love instead of lack.

From Storms to Stillness

Sometimes the greatest storms reveal the greatest gift: knowing your Shepherd is near. *"Peace, be still"* is not merely His words—it is His rhythm. Every step beside still waters begins with that sacred sound, the heartbeat of Heaven whispering peace into your chaos.

The Shepherd leads you through turbulence—pain, trauma, anxiety, fatigue—not to expose your weakness, but to reveal His nearness. He rests His hand upon your heart and whispers, *You no longer have to let storms rule over you. I am here. I am with you. I am Peace.*

"And the peace of God, which surpasses all understanding, will guard your hearts and your minds in Christ Jesus." — Philippians 4:7

This peace is not passive; it is powerful. It is a weapon in the hands of your Shepherd King, and He has placed it in yours. *"I leave the gift of peace with you—My peace. Not the kind of fragile peace given by the world, but My perfect peace. Don't yield to fear or be troubled in your hearts—instead, be courageous!"* (John 14:27 TPT).

The peace of God is not fragile—it conquers. *"And the God of peace will swiftly pound Satan to a pulp under your feet!"* (Romans 16:20 TPT). Peace be still. God of peace. Grace and peace—multiplied to you (2 Peter 1:2).

In every storm of life, there is an invitation: a sacred opportunity for stillness. The Shepherd's leading beside still waters is not forceful but tender. He never compels you to drink, yet His heart longs for you to taste and see His peace. *"Taste and see that the Lord is good; blessed is the one who takes refuge in Him"* (Psalm 34:8).

Peace is your portion. It is not something you earn; it is something He already paid for. *"He was wounded for our transgressions... the chastisement for our peace was upon Him"* (Isaiah 53:5). Peace is not the absence of storms; it is the presence of your Shepherd. He was chastised for your peace so you would never face chaos without this holy weapon.

Let the same voice that once calmed the sea calm your soul again today: *Peace, be still.* And as He whispers peace into your storm, He leads you gently toward the still waters—where your soul learns that true calm is not found in the silence of the waves, but in the presence of the Shepherd who walks upon them (John 6:16–21).

The Motivation of Stillness

When the Shepherd leads you beside still waters, He invites you to drink His peace. *"All you thirsty ones, come to me... and drink... so that rivers of living water will burst out from within you"* (John 7:37–38 TPT). These waters aren't stagnant pools; they are living streams—clear, refreshing, endless.

Here, fear no longer drives you; perfect love leads you (1 John 4:18). Your life was never meant to be powered by panic, striving, or trauma triggers. The Shepherd leads, and you choose to bend low and drink (James 4:6). In His stillness, peace becomes your portion, safety your shelter, and renewal your river. He wants your life motivated not by frenzy, but by love—a love that quenches, satisfies, and overflows.

Love's Lasting Motivation: 15 Healthy Motivators

1. Affirmation → not Anxiety: "I am my beloved's, and His desire is for me." → Security replaces striving. (Song of Songs 7:10)

2. Encouragement → not Expectation: "Encourage one another and build each other up." → Love inspires, not demands. (1 Thessalonians 5:11)

3. Security → not Striving: "Be still and know that I am God." → Rest becomes strength. (Psalm 46:10)

4. Love → not Fear: "Perfect love casts out fear." → His love removes all torment. (1 John 4:18)

5. Joy → not Pressure: "In His presence is fullness of joy." → Delight replaces duty. (Psalm 16:11; Nehemiah 8:10)

6. Peace → not Panic: "The peace of God guards your hearts and minds." → Calm replaces chaos. (Philippians 4:7)

7. Patience → not Perfectionism: "The Lord is good to those who wait for Him." → Trust replaces timelines. (Lamentations 3:25)

8. Kindness → not People-Pleasing: "Do to others as you would have them do to you." → Compassion replaces performance. (Luke 6:31)

9. Goodness → not Guilt: "Surely goodness and mercy will follow me." → Grace overtakes shame. (Psalm 23:6)

10. Faithfulness → not Fear of Failure: "Great is Your faithfulness." → Consistency replaces comparison. (Lamentations 3:23)

11. Gentleness → not Judgment: "Let your gentleness be evident to all." → Mercy triumphs over judgment. (Philippians 4:5; James 2:13)

12. Self-Control → not Self-Protection: "God gave us a spirit of power, love, and self-control." → Boundaries rooted in love, not fear. (2 Timothy 1:7)

13. Abundance → not Scarcity: "My God will supply all your needs." → Provision silences panic. (Philippians 4:19)

14. Identity → not Insecurity: "See what great love the Father has lavished on us." → Belonging replaces proving. (1 John 3:1)

15. Trust → not Trauma: "Trust in the Lord with all your heart..." → Surrender heals what control cannot. (Proverbs 3:5–6)

"The fruit of righteousness will be peace; its effect will be quietness and confidence forever." (Isaiah 32:17)

The momentum you really want starts in the stillness of His presence—by the waters of life where your soul stops spinning and starts drinking.

"You will be like a well-watered garden, like a spring whose waters never fail." (Isaiah 58:11)

The Spirit Over the Deep

Still waters are not shallow—they are sacred depths. In the beginning, *"Darkness was over the surface of the deep, and the Spirit of God was hovering over the waters"* (Genesis 1:2). Where the world saw chaos, God saw a canvas. The Spirit hovered, brooded, prepared—and He does the same with you.

When the Shepherd leads you beside still waters, He isn't ignoring your pain. He is hovering over your chaos with tender love. *"The Lord your God is in your midst... He will quiet you with His love"* (Zephaniah 3:17). He is not afraid of your deep places. He broods over your grief (Psalm 34:18), hovers over your confusion (Isaiah 42:16), and shines into your shadows (John 1:5).

Still waters are where your soul is re-created—gently renewed—where hidden, hurting places are restored by His marvelous light (1 Peter 2:9). The spaces you surrendered to silence are sacred to Him, places for a breathtaking exchange (Isaiah 61:3): ashes become beauty, chaos becomes a canvas, darkness becomes dawn. By His creative power, what felt lifeless breathes again—whole and wonder-filled (Ezekiel 37:4–6; 2 Corinthians 5:17).

"For God, who said, 'Let light shine out of darkness,' made His light shine in our hearts..." — 2 Corinthians 4:6

Menuchah: The Resting Place

The Hebrew word for still is **Menuchah**—'a resting place, an oasis, a settled quietness.' Not passive. Not empty. Rich, fertile ground for restoration. *"I will refresh the weary and satisfy the faint"* (Jeremiah 31:25).

When the Shepherd leads you beside still waters, He's leading you into restoration (Psalm 23:3), healing (Jeremiah 17:14), quiet confidence (Isaiah 32:17), all things new (2 Corinthians 5:17), and a home where you belong (Exodus 33:14). He doesn't just calm your situation—He calms your soul (Philippians 4:7).

The War Between Hurry and Stillness

Hurry is fear in motion—holy hustle's counterfeit. It's the illusion of importance masking the infection of insecurity. *"Martha, Martha... you are worried and upset about many things, but few things are needed"* (Luke 10:41–42). Stillness speaks a better word: you already have what you need (Psalm 23:1). You are safe in your Shepherd's arms (Proverbs 18:10). You are led, not lost (Romans 8:14).

Stillness is your weapon against scarcity, your rebuke to the rush. *"Yes, God is more than ready to overwhelm you with every form of grace... He will make you overflow with abundance..."* (2 Corinthians 9:8 TPT). The *"few things"* become One thing when you sit at the feet of your Shepherd—simply being present in His presence.

You don't have to impress Him with prepping. He isn't moved by performance; He is moved by your presence. You don't have to keep preparing for His arrival—He has already prepared a place for you. *"I go to prepare a place for you..."* (John 14:2–3 TPT).

So exhale. The Shepherd isn't waiting for you to earn an invitation; He's waiting for you to simply sit down. *"Surrender your anxiety! Be silent and stop your striving..."* (Psalm 46:10 TPT). *"Relax and rest... for the Lord rewards fully those who simply trust Him"* (Psalm 116:7 TPT).

Stillness is not the absence of movement; it is the presence of trust (Proverbs 3:5–6). And when trust leads, hurry loses its power.

When Frustration Replaces Stillness

Frustration is often the first sign you've been dislodged from the waters of peace. It grows where stillness has been replaced by striving. Give away your peace, and you'll begin to react instead of respond. You'll feel powerless—and powerlessness breeds victimhood. You'll live blaming outward instead of tending inward. *"Each heart knows its own bitterness..."* (Proverbs 14:10). *"Above all else, guard your heart..."* (Proverbs 4:23).

Stillness isn't weakness—it is awareness. And frustration, when filtered through grace, becomes a holy invitation to return to the Shepherd's leading.

External frustrations will always exist—storms, disappointments, misunderstandings, unmet expectations. But the true battle is never *"out there."* Outside problems rarely heal the inside ache. Blaming others might feel justified for a moment, but it leaves the soul bound.

When the posture of your heart shifts from outward to inward—from accusation to cultivation—you'll find the Shepherd waiting. He never called you to be tossed by the winds of circumstance, but to walk in the calm authority of His presence.

"I leave the gift of peace with you—My peace..." (John 14:27 TPT). *"In this unbelieving world you will experience trouble and sorrows... but I have conquered the world!"* (John 16:33 TPT).

Victimhood whispers, *You are powerless.* Royalty whispers back, *You are seated with Him in heavenly places* (Ephesians 2:6). When the Good Shepherd cultivates your heart, frustration becomes formation. Stillness becomes strength. Surrender creates a wake of opportunity where problems transform into promises and failures become fertile soil for creativity.

So be of good cheer—your Shepherd has overcome the world. And when your soul stays anchored in His peace, even chaos becomes a current that carries you closer, not away, but to His heart.

The Living Water Exchange

At a well in Samaria, Jesus asked a woman, *"Will you give Me a drink?"* (John 4:7). What does it mean when the Source of Living Water asks you for a drink? It means your presence satisfies Him. Your surrendered soul becomes His refreshment—not your performance, but your presence.

Later He told His disciples, *"I have food to eat that you don't know about"* (John 4:32). His nourishment? Connection. Communion. Stillness with you. He is fed by fellowship—filled by love returned. *"For God is*

Spirit, and those who worship Him must worship in the realm of the Spirit and in truth" (John 4:24 TPT).

She came to draw ordinary water and encountered the Well Himself. He offered her water that would never run dry, and she found the One who knew her completely—yet loved her still. *"Believe in Me so that rivers of living water will burst out from within you..."* (John 7:38 TPT).

This is the secret of true worship: it isn't bound by place, performance, or perfection. It is anchored in Spirit and Truth. The weary find rest not by striving to reach Him, but by realizing He's already sitting beside them, waiting to be known.

"Simply join your life with Mine... You will find refreshment and rest in Me." — Matthew 11:28–29 (TPT)

In holy mystery, you become His resting place even as He becomes yours. The Living Water you long for is the same Love that longs for you.

Drink deeply today.

Soul Activation

Hover, Heal, and Be Still

Picture yourself at the edge of still waters. The Shepherd stands beside you, and the Holy Spirit hovers over the depths—tender, brooding, present. Hear Him whisper, *I see your innermost places. I know your wounds. I am hovering over your chaos to bring beauty. You are not forsaken. You are My beloved* (Psalm 139:13–18).

Now picture the storm that's been raging within you—the crashing waves of worry, fear, or fatigue. The Shepherd lifts His hand and speaks the same words that once stilled the sea: *"Peace, be still"* (Mark 4:39). Feel the wind quiet. Feel the waters settle. The same voice that commands the storm now calms your soul, and the battle within begins to bow to His peace.

Now pause. Where has frustration spoken louder than peace? Let Him show you where you gave away your power, and let Him return you to stillness.

Watch the water shimmer. Light breaks in. Creation begins again. *"If anyone is in Christ, he is a new creation..."* (2 Corinthians 5:17). Breathe deep. Drink the stillness. Let His *Peace, be still* echo through your heart until the storm within and around you yields to His voice.

Let Him lead you here for a drink—again and again.

Journal Prompts

1. **Where have I mistaken busyness for faithfulness, and what is Jesus revealing about my true motivations?** (Luke 10:41–42; Proverbs 16:2)

2. **What has been fueling my momentum — fear or presence — and how is perfect love inviting me into a different way?** (1 John 4:18; Proverbs 16:2)

3. **How does my perspective shift when I remember that peace is not only the presence of my Shepherd in the storm, but also a weapon He's placed in my hands?** (John 14:27; Philippians 4:7; Romans 16:20)

4. **Where have I given away my peace and allowed frustration or hurry to lead — and what invitation is Jesus giving me to return to rest?** (Proverbs 14:10; Isaiah 30:15)

5. **What would choosing stillness look like in this season, and how might it realign my heart, pace, and priorities?** (Psalm 46:10; Psalm 23:2)

6. **What deep places in me is the Holy Spirit hovering over — brooding with love, preparing to bring beauty from chaos?** (Genesis 1:2; Isaiah 61:3)

7. How does it change my understanding of God — and my relationship with Him — to realize that my presence actually refreshes His heart? (John 4:32)

Now Declaration

My Great Shepherd takes the lead.

I am led beside still waters. The Shepherd draws me into rest, not rush. (Psalm 23:2)

I am created for stillness; my soul thrives in quiet trust, not frantic striving. (Isaiah 30:15)

I am nourished by His presence and being present, not pressure; I move from peace, not panic. (Philippians 4:7)

I am aware of the Spirit's hovering; even over my chaos, He broods with love and purpose. (Genesis 1:2)

I am not driven by fear — I am anchored in joy; He silences every voice but His own. (1 John 4:18)

I am a well-watered garden; I drink deeply of His living water and bear lasting fruit. (Isaiah 58:11; John 7:38)

I am a carrier of divine calm; stillness clothes me with His strength. (Psalm 46:10)

I am empowered to reclaim my peace; I guard my heart and return to rest. (Proverbs 4:23)

I am the delight of the Shepherd; He leads me gently and enjoys stillness with me. (Psalm 16:11)

I am whole. I am home. I am His. My soul is settled, safe, and satisfied in Him. (2 Corinthians 5:17)

Final Reflection

The Stillness That Leads

Stillness is where the Shepherd's voice becomes clear again.

He leads you here — not to pause your purpose, but to restore your peace.

Stillness is not the absence of motion — it's the awareness of His presence and the flow of His authority within you.

Your Shepherd slows your hurried heart until you can hear His whisper again.

He calms your chaos, not by control, but by companionship.

The same Spirit who hovered over the deep now hovers over you — bringing beauty from brokenness, and calm from within.

Even in the fiercest storm, His stillness remains. He stands within your waves and speaks, *"Peace, be still."*

And because you belong to Him, His authority becomes your inheritance.

You are not powerless before the wind — you carry the voice that silences it.

Here, by still waters, you remember what peace sounds like.

You remember who He is — and who you are in Him.

The Shepherd's stillness doesn't remove the storm — it transforms it into revelation.

This is where striving surrenders to trust, where chaos bows to calm, and your soul learns to simply be.

He leadeth me beside still waters.

Chapter 5
He Restoreth My Soul
Psalm 23:3a

The Shepherd of the Soul

There is no wound too deep (Psalm 147:3), no fracture too hidden (Hebrews 4:13), and no history too tangled for His redeeming love (Romans 8:28). Before you ever reached for Him, He was already reaching for you. The Shepherd has never turned away from the hidden and hurting places. His compassion doesn't recoil—it reaches relentlessly deeper.

He walks through the ruins without flinching, gathering what others called broken. Every scar becomes a story of His faithfulness, every wound an entry point for glory. He enters the secret gardens, the shadowed valleys, the tangled wilderness of your heart—even the hidden chambers of your soul (Psalm 139:1–3)—and with infinite patience begins the holy work of restoration (Philippians 1:6).

Religion may whisper, *Clean yourself up before you come.* But grace says, *Come, and I will make you clean* (John 15:3).

Our attempts at righteousness are tattered garments—thin threads of striving, fig-leaf coverings like Adam and Eve's first attempt to hide, unable to conceal the weight of shame (Genesis 3:7). Isaiah saw it clearly:

even our best efforts are "like the soiled cloth of a woman's cycle" (Isaiah 64:6)—unclean and unable to make us whole. But now, through faith in Jesus, something far greater has happened. What once was stained has been exchanged. The gospel singing a better song: come as you are.

"Our faith in Jesus transfers God's righteousness to us, and He now declares us flawless in His eyes." — Romans 5:1 (TPT)

No longer clothed in self-effort, we wear the seamless robe of His perfection. The stains of striving have been erased and replaced by the brilliance of His grace.

"Could it be any clearer that our former identity is now and forever deprived of its power? For we were co-crucified with Him to dismantle the stronghold of sin within us..." — Romans 6:6 (TPT)

We do not stand before God in our own virtue but in His. Our righteousness is not something earned—it is Someone received. His name is Jesus, and He has become our garment of glory. And this same Shepherd who robes us in righteousness also restores what sin and sorrow once shattered. He Himself is our cleansing. His presence—not our striving—heals fractures, silences shame, and renews what was broken.

Our Great Shepherd has already done it all. His blood spilled on the ground speaks a better word—reconciliation (Hebrews 12:24). His cross reconnected us to the Father—the very Father who was in Christ reconciling the world to Himself, even while we were still sinners (2 Corinthians 5:19; Romans 5:8).

Yet there are moments when the noise of life grows louder than His voice, when thoughts drain your hope, joy feels thin, and peace seems far away.

Old wounds whisper again, trying to convince you nothing has changed. But those memories are not masters; they are only lying vanities (Jonah 2:8). Recognize them for what they are: shadows without substance, faint echoes of a defeated enemy.

Like Jonah, you may feel tossed about—swallowed by circumstance, sitting in the dark belly of disappointment. But even here, His grace whispers authority and stillness into your soul. The same Word that calmed the sea now speaks through you: *"Let God be true, and every man a liar"* (Romans 3:4). Every accusation and every shame-soaked memory must bow to the truth of His Word.

Take each thought captive (2 Corinthians 10:5). Hold it to the light of the cross, and worship right there in the storm. As you lift your voice—not in denial but in trust—you will sense something sacred shifting. What once felt like the belly of despair becomes the birthplace of new life. Darkness loosens its grip. Morning light begins to break through.

For the Word made flesh still heals the human heart and still breathes life where there was none. So breathe in grace. Let peace settle over you. Rest in the presence of the One who restores all things. Let God be true, and let every circumstance that exalts itself above His presence be revealed as a shadow with no substance.

You were not made for torment—you were made for wonder. Not for striving, but for belonging. Your life is now hidden with Christ in God (Colossians 3:3 TPT). When you surrender to His presence over your pain, everything shifts. You rise from depths to solid ground, from confusion to clarity, from survival to singing (Psalm 103).

There is no barrier He has not already broken, no distance He has not already crossed. Before you behaved, you were chosen. Before you believed, you were called His own (Judges 6:12). He first loved you (1 John 4:19). You were always known (Jeremiah 29:11), always pursued (Psalm 136), always wanted (Isaiah 30:18). At the cross, His love found you and forever claimed you.

So when condemnation or delay whispers otherwise, remember: every "not yet" and every "not enough" is just another lying vanity (Romans 8:1). The Shepherd has already led you out, and His truth will always lead you home (John 14:2-3).

You Are His Treasure

In the beginning, clay met Creator. From the ground, the hands of Glory shaped humanity—fragile, earthy, and breathtakingly intentional. Then God leaned close, and the breath of Heaven filled the dirt. Dust became a reservoir for divine habitation. The infinite chose to dwell in the finite. We were made of earth, yet destined for glory—molded in His image, formed to be carriers of His presence, earthen vessels shining with Eternal Light.

"For God, who said, 'Let brilliant light shine out of darkness,' is the one who has cascaded his light into us..." — 2 Corinthians 4:6 (TPT)

Every vessel is shaped from the same dust and filled with a unique facet of His glory. And the purpose of that glory is not to elevate the vessel, but to reveal the Treasure within. All the light, all the beauty, all the transformation—it is from Him, through Him, and unto Him.

Jesus told a parable of a man who stumbled upon a treasure so priceless he sold everything just to make it his. The Great Shepherd is that Man—and you, dirt and all, are the treasure hidden in the field of your own story.

But here is the miracle wrapped in mystery: He didn't only purchase the treasure. He bought the whole field. Every inch of soil, every hidden layer, every unrefined corner, every buried memory. He redeemed the dirt as well as the treasure within—the mess and the miracle. Nothing in your story was too buried for His love to claim. He saw treasure where others saw dirt. He saw your dazzling beauty beneath the dust. And He paid the highest price imaginable—His own blood.

Jesus did not die for junk. He didn't go to the cross hoping you might be worth it. He went because Heaven already decided you are. The value of a thing is determined by the price someone is willing to pay—and the Son of God deemed you priceless (John 3:16–17).

"It is the glory of God to conceal a matter, and the glory of kings to search it out." — Proverbs 25:2

Even now, the Spirit leads you to uncover what Heaven hid within you—divine treasure wrapped in human form. The Shepherd's work is always preparation for glory. He is polishing, refining, and revealing, not to erase your humanity but to let His divinity shine through it.

You are not the source of the glory—you are the showcase of it (Colossians 1:27). You are not the light—you carry the Light (Matthew 5:14; John 8:12). And when the world sees radiance shining through your cracks and scars, they glorify your Father in Heaven (Matthew 5:16).

You are dust kissed by Deity—the mingling place of Heaven and Earth. The treasure and the field. The vessel housing the glory. Grace is the hand that digs through the soil of shame to reveal Heaven's hidden wealth.

So let Him embrace you with the depths of His love. Let Him breathe restoration into your weary soul. Let His fullness fill you (Ephesians 2:1 TPT). Your only role is to yield—let Him. Trust that His Word washing over you is stronger than every thought of accusation that tries to drown you (Ephesians 5:26).

What Is the Soul?

You are not a random cluster of thoughts and emotions. You are a masterpiece, woven together by divine hands (Psalm 139:14). You were created as a triune being—spirit, soul, and body—bearing the image of our Triune God (1 Thessalonians 5:23).

Your spirit communes with God, awakened in new birth (John 3:6). Yet even before you were born again, He was pursuing you—whispering, drawing you with everlasting love (Jeremiah 31:3). New birth awakens you to a reality you can't unsee: He was never absent, even when you felt all alone (Acts 17:27–28).

Your soul is the garden of mind, will, emotions, imagination, and memory—the place where thoughts grow and dreams are planted (Psalm 42:11). Your body is the temple that carries both spirit and soul, sacred to God (1 Corinthians 6:19).

But false leaven tries to creep in. Gnosticism still whispers its ancient lie: that deeper mystery and harder striving unlock greater portals of blessing. Grace exposes the illusion. The only mystery worth beholding is the Lamb—His wounds, the true portals of glory. Through the holes in His hands, feet, and side, Heaven poured itself out and declared: *It is finished.* No secret knowledge can surpass what love has already accomplished.

Dualism poisons the mind into believing your spirit is good but your body and soul are disposable. Both are lies. Jesus came in the flesh and dwelt among us (John 1:14). He embraced the fullness of our humanity. The disciples said, *"We touched Him... we handled the Word of Life,"* and now that same Word holds you. He delights in every part of you—spirit, soul, and body. The gospel does not teach escapism; it teaches resurrection and restoration (Colossians 1:20).

In Hebrew thought, the soul—**Nephesh**—is not a fragment but the whole living being: breath, life, self (Genesis 2:7). To dishonor your body or diminish your soul is to dishonor the very temple where God has chosen to dwell.

Let me say it plainly: the gospel is no tale of escapism. Death is not our savior, nor the doorway we long for. The only true escape—the Way—is the rescuing power of our Great Shepherd King, delivering us from sin, death, and eternal ruin. Restoration is not escape. It is resurrection (Colossians 3:1–2 TPT).

Restoration Is More Than Repair

When the Shepherd restores, He does not merely patch what is broken. He does not polish what has been shattered. The Hebrew word **Shuv** is rich with promise: 'to return, to bring back, to turn again to the very beginning'—to the intent that has never wavered in the heart of God (Jeremiah 30:17).

Restoration with God is not cosmetic repair. It is resurrection (Romans 6:4).

Let this truth resonate in the depths of your soul. Let resurrection life rise within you until it reshapes your every breath, becoming the rhythm of your being—the steady pulse of Heaven in your chest.

You are not a fixer-upper. You are the garden of God that He dreamed of before time began. Before foundations were laid, before light broke into darkness, the Lamb was slain for you (Revelation 13:8). His thoughts toward you have always been thick with hope (Jeremiah 29:11). And by His Spirit, He does not merely tape together broken walls—He replants Eden within you, streams of living water flowing, your soul restored afresh, brand new, your life becoming His favored dwelling place (Isaiah 58:11).

Kainos vs. Neos: The Beauty of New Creation

"If anyone is in Christ, he is a new creation; the old has passed away, behold, the new has come." — 2 Corinthians 5:17

In Greek, "new" here is: **Kainos (καινός)**—'new in kind, unprecedented, never seen before, of a higher quality.' It is different from neos, which simply means new in time.

You are not just an upgraded version of your old self. You are a kainos creation—reborn from Heaven's order, raised with Christ into a life the world has never seen before (Romans 8:11; Revelation 21:5). Where the world sees ruins, He sees wellsprings (John 4:14). Where the world counts loss, He multiplies life (John 10:10). Your destiny is kainos: resurrected, restored, radiant.

Anakainōsis: Becoming What You Already Are

"Stop imitating the ideals and opinions of the culture around you, but be inwardly transformed by the Holy Spirit through a total reformation of how you think..." — Romans 12:2 (TPT)

"Do not be conformed to this world, but be transformed by the renewing of your mind..." — Romans 12:2 (NASB)

The word for "renewing" is: **Anakainōsis (ἀνακαίνωσις)**: *'ana*—again, upward, back to; *kainos*—new in kind, unprecedented, superior.'

Anakainōsis is not self-help or religious behavior modification. It is not mustering mental strength or fixing yourself through soul-power. You were never asked to renew your mind alone. It is yielding to the indwelling Holy Spirit—your Paraklētos—Helper, Comforter, Teacher, Advocate, and so much more.

It is the Spirit of God reshaping you from within, the privilege of divine partnership restoring what was always meant to be. You are not striving to become new; you are learning to live from what already happened. Your spirit already knows the truth—anakainōsis is your soul catching up. It is the Spirit uprooting old lies, planting holy thoughts, and reforming your inner world to mirror your heavenly identity (Romans 12:2; 2 Corinthians 4:16). Each moment of surrender becomes another wave of anakainōsis—a holy reformation of the way you think.

The Holy Spirit in the Garden of Your Soul

The Spirit is not a guest—He is a Gardener. He dwells, tends, and cultivates (1 Corinthians 3:16). He uproots weeds of bitterness and fear (Hebrews 12:15). He plants seeds of joy and righteousness (Galatians 6:8). He waters dry ground with living streams (Isaiah 44:3). He shines light where shadows once reigned (Malachi 4:2). The same Spirit who hovered over the chaos of Genesis now hovers over you—not to condemn, but to cultivate; not to demand, but to dwell.

"I will put My Spirit in you, and you will live." — Ezekiel 37:14

Just as He hovered over the deep and spoke light into darkness, He does the same with you. He is not afraid of the places you've hidden—the memories you buried, the pain you learned to survive instead of heal. What if *"Let there be light"* was never meant to expose you—but to heal you? (Genesis 1:2)

The Soil of Your Soul

The Holy Spirit does not enter your soul like a critic with a clipboard. He comes like a gardener—with patience, tenderness, and truth. Jesus did not distance Himself from human pain. He stepped into it. *"The Word became flesh and dwelt among us."* (John 1:14) He knows sorrow. He knows grief. He knows exhaustion. Not theoretically—but personally. He is *"a Man of sorrows, acquainted with grief."* (Isaiah 53:3) So when the Spirit tends the garden of your soul, He does not rush you past what hurts. He goes with you into it. Healing is not erasing the past. Healing is allowing love to interrupt it. Some wounds no longer shout. They whisper—quietly shaping reactions, relationships, rest, and trust. This is where the Holy Spirit begins—not by shaming what's there, but by gently tilling the soil.

When the Spirit Tills the Soil

1. Where the Soul Learned to Stay Guarded

Some of what exhausts you began as protection. Constant vigilance. Subtle anxiety. Control disguised as responsibility. At one time, being alert kept you safe. But what once protected you may now be draining you. The Holy Spirit does not rip these roots out. He asks, *"What are you still guarding yourself against?"* And then He stays—teaching your soul that it is no longer alone.

2. Where the Soul Carries Too Much

You can be functioning and still be deeply tired. That kind of fatigue doesn't come from doing too much—it comes from carrying too much. Unprocessed grief. Unspoken fear. Worth tied to performance. The Spirit does not demand more fruit. He says, *"Let Me carry what you were never meant to hold."* Because fruit grows naturally in rested soil—it is never forced.

3. Where the Soul Hid to Survive

Shame convinces you to hide—not because you're bad, but because you learned it was safer to be unseen. So you manage appearances. You silence parts of yourself. You disconnect to cope. But shame cannot survive where love stays. The Holy Spirit does not recoil from what you buried. He kneels beside it. Names it. And covers it—not with secrecy, but with grace.

The Invitation

The garden of your soul holds both weeds and treasures. Both grief and gold. Both pain and promise. And the Holy Spirit is faithful to tend it all. Not to make you perfect. But to make you whole. Not to strip away your humanity. But to restore it. Because the One who formed your soul is the same One who is still—patiently, lovingly—tending every detail...So you can live fully, not just survive.

Soul Activation

Return and Be Made New

Picture your soul as a garden—some parts blooming, some barren, some tangled and forgotten.

See the Shepherd step through the gate (John 10:9). He carries no judgment, only tenderness (Matthew 11:29). He kneels beside what you've buried and plants new seeds with His own hands (Psalm 126:5). He waters dry soil with tears of love (Psalm 56:8). He breathes, and kainos life stirs from the ground.

Hear Him whisper, *"Behold, I make all things new"* (Revelation 21:5). *"You are My garden, My delight"* (Song of Songs 4:12). *"Nothing is too lost for Me to restore"* (Jeremiah 30:17).

Let His presence soak your roots like spring rain (Hosea 6:3). Let your soul bloom again. You are not just better. You are brand new.

Close your eyes, and let the eyes of your understanding imagine this beautiful truth.

Journal Prompts

1. **Where have I believed parts of my soul were too broken or too far gone for true restoration, and what is Jesus saying about those places?** (Psalm 147:3; Jeremiah 30:17)

2. **What is the Holy Spirit planting in the garden of my soul in this season — what new desires, truths, or dreams?** (Galatians 6:8–9; Psalm 126:5)

3. **What would it feel like to fully agree with Heaven's verdict: *"I am not a fixer-upper; I am a new (kainos) creation?"*** (2 Corinthians 5:17)

4. **Where have I unknowingly tried to *"fix myself"* or renew my mind in my own strength, instead of partnering with the Spirit's grace?** (Zechariah 4:6; Romans 12:2)

5. **How can I practically surrender, today, to the Holy Spirit's daily work of anakainōsis — letting Him reshape how I think and feel?** (Romans 12:2; 2 Corinthians 4:16)

6. **Which old lies about my worth, story, or identity is the Shepherd inviting me to uproot so He can replant truth?** (Jonah 2:8; 2 Corinthians 10:5)

7. **Where do I already see signs of His restoration — places in my soul that are more alive, at peace, or hopeful than they used to be?** (Psalm 23:3; Philippians 1:6)

Now Declaration

The Restoration of the Soul

I am a new creation — *kainos,* not improved, but entirely reborn. (2 Corinthians 5:17)

I am restored — spirit, soul, and body — by the Shepherd who never stops pursuing me. (Psalm 23:3, 1 Thessalonians 5:23)

I am rooted in divine love and nourished by Heaven's peace. (Ephesians 3:17, Isaiah 58:11)

I am the garden of God — cultivated by the Spirit, blooming with purpose. (Song of Songs 4:12, 1 Corinthians 3:16)

I am being renewed day by day — transformed by His presence and truth. (2 Corinthians 4:16, Romans 12:2)

I am no longer bound by what was broken. I live from my identity Heaven has spoken. (Jeremiah 30:17, Isaiah 61:3)

I am aligned with the mind of Christ. My thoughts are being made new to match who I already am in Him. (1 Corinthians 2:16, Romans 12:2)

I am filled with resurrection life. The same Spirit that raised Christ is rewriting every part of me. (Romans 8:11, Ezekiel 37:14)

I am who He says I am — restored, radiant, righteous, and rejoicing. (Colossians 2:10, Isaiah 60:1)

Final Reflection

The Restoration of the Soul

Restoration is not repair — it's resurrection.

The Shepherd breathes life where hope once faded.

He steps into the quiet garden of your soul, turning hidden wounds into holy ground.

You are not being fixed — you are being made new.

This is kainos life: not improved, but reborn.

The Spirit still hovers, replanting beauty where ashes were. Here, your striving ceases.

Here, your soul breathes again. Here, the Shepherd restores your soul. He restoreth my soul.

Chapter 6

He Leadeth Me in Paths of Righteousness for His Name's Sake

Psalm 23:3b

He Leads You

"*He leads me in paths of righteousness for His name's sake.*" — Psalm 23:3

This is not a casual phrase. It is the beating heart of the Shepherd's mission—to lead you. Not push you. Not pressure you. Not manipulate or coerce. He leads you—gently, purposefully, faithfully—toward a destination He Himself has already prepared.

We were never designed to figure everything out on our own. You were not created to blaze trails by sheer will or wander endlessly in the wilderness of self-direction. You were born to be led. Your soul was fashioned for the cadence of His footsteps. The most powerful and liberating act you will ever take is not striving harder, but surrendering deeper—trusting the Shepherd who knows the way home.

But this invites a searching question, one that determines the trajectory of your life: **Who or what is leading you?** Because someone—or something—always is. Fear can lead. Shame can lead. Culture, ambition, trauma, unforgiveness, bitterness—each carves out its own path. Yet none of them lead to life.

Only one Shepherd has gone before you and prepared a way that ends in wholeness, righteousness, and home. And when He leads, He does not point vaguely toward a destination and leave you to navigate the terrain. He walks before you, clearing obstacles, cutting through darkness, making a way where there was none.

The Hebrew word for lead in Psalm 23:3—**Nāḥâ**—carries far more depth than mere direction. It means: 'to guide with care, to bring gently, to conduct along a path already prepared.' It paints the image of a shepherd going before his flock, scanning the road ahead, removing thorns and stones so that every step is sure and safe. This is not leadership from a distance; it is companionship in motion.

When the Lord leads, the path is not theoretical—it is already carved. And that carving was not done with a staff or shovel, but with a spear, with your destiny written on it.

The Path Carved by Love

The moment the spear pierced the side of our Savior-Shepherd (John 19:34), a pathway was literally cut open—straight to the heart of God. Imagine the holy irony: hatred carving the path that would lead to eternal love. Human rage tearing into divine mercy, and mercy responding not with wrath, but with reconciliation.

As flesh split and the spear reached His heart, blood and water poured forth—the twin rivers of cleansing and new birth. This was not random. This was Heaven's map being drawn into the soil of the earth. The blood cried out a better word than vengeance (Hebrews 12:24). The water marked the washing of renewal (Titus 3:5). Together, they did more than forgive you—they forged a way into the very heart of God.

This is the movement of the gospel: from revenge to reconciliation, from separation to belonging, from condemnation to covenant. The path is not one you must fight to earn; it is one that was fought for you. So when the Shepherd says, *Follow Me,* it is not a vague invitation. It is a summons to walk a trail that cuts straight through death itself and emerges into resurrection life—into safety, intimacy, and identity.

The Righteousness of Your Shepherd King

You were never meant to wander through life guessing your worth (Jeremiah 1:5). You were never designed to drift in the shifting sands of identity confusion (Ephesians 1:4–5). You were created to walk righteous paths—paths anchored in the unbreakable, covenantal love of your Shepherd King (Romans 8:38–39).

And here is the breathtaking truth: *"You are the righteousness of God in Christ Jesus"* (2 Corinthians 5:21). Not by striving (Ephesians 2:8–9). Not by perfection (Romans 4:5). But by grace (2 Corinthians 12:9), by blood (Hebrews 10:19–22), by His name (Philippians 2:9–10).

Your Shepherd has draped you in His righteousness, clothed you in royal garments (Isaiah 61:10), and now leads you daily on paths paved with His perfection (Psalm 85:13). These are not paths of moral performance or religious achievement. They are highways of grace—ancient roads where mercy walks beside justice, and every step declares the nature of the One who leads you.

Grace is not permission to live less; it is power to live as you were always meant to. It doesn't lower the standard; it fills you with the life of the One who already met it. Grace does not say, *Try harder.* It whispers, *Abide deeper* (John 15:4–11).

When you walk in grace, you walk in the strength of Another. His righteousness becomes your rhythm. His obedience becomes your overflow. *"For it is God who works in you both to will and to do His good pleasure"* (Philippians 2:13). The Shepherd's paths are not paved with performance but with Presence—roads of restoration where divine life flows through human vessels, empowering what self-effort never could.

Grace-Empowered Righteous Living

Righteousness is not merely a legal status; it is a living flow of grace. It is Heaven's favor saturating your life, realigning your desires, and transforming your nature from the inside out (Galatians 2:20).

Abraham's faith was credited to him as righteousness (Romans 4:3), not because of perfect behavior, but because he believed God. Let these two words settle deep in your soul: **only believe** (Mark 5:36). Faith opened the door, and grace did the transforming.

Grace is not passive tolerance; it is divine empowerment. *"For the grace of God has appeared, bringing salvation to all people. It teaches us… to live self-controlled, upright, and godly lives"* (Titus 2:11–12). Grace does not wink at sin; it liberates you from its power. It does not tell you to try harder; it infuses you with divine strength. Where your strength ends, grace begins (Joel 3:10).

When Paul wrestled with weakness, the Lord answered, *"My grace is sufficient for you, for My power is made perfect in weakness"* (2 Corinthians 12:9). Every weakness bows to the sufficiency of His grace. Grace doesn't give permission to live however you want—it transforms your want. It reshapes desire to mirror His righteousness, drawing you upward into the life you were made for.

Through grace, you don't just believe in righteousness—you begin to walk it out. Because of Jesus—your Firstborn Shepherd King—the favor of His name has become your inheritance (Romans 8:29–30). And as you walk in that inheritance, every step becomes an expression of His nature: His character (Colossians 3:12), His goodness (Psalm 23:6), His authority (Luke 10:19), His workmanship (Ephesians 2:10).

Grace-fueled obedience begins to say what your soul once forgot: *I am not lost—I am led. I am not striving—I am strengthened. I am not bound—I am becoming. I am walking in righteousness for His name's sake.*

And when you fall, you rise again. *"A righteous man falls seven times and rises again"* (Proverbs 24:16). Shame does not get to rule your heart or spiral you into regret. In a heartbeat, you remember who you truly are—beloved son, cherished daughter. Choose conviction, not condemnation (Romans 8:1). Yesterday's failure does not define today's identity. Grace rewrites your story in real time.

You were never meant to wallow or wander. You were made to walk, to rise, and to go from glory to glory (2 Corinthians 3:18). Even in weakness, His strength is made perfect (2 Corinthians 12:9).

His Name Is Now Your Name

"He leads me in paths of righteousness for His name's sake." — Psalm 23:3

Not because you earned it, but because He sealed it.

In ancient covenant culture, names were everything. To act for one's name's sake meant to act with the full weight of one's identity, honor, and legacy. When God leads you, He does so not merely as a guide, but as a Father whose reputation is bound up in your journey. His faithfulness to you is a reflection of His name.

And in Christ, that name has now become yours. *"I will write on them the name of My God... and My own new name"* (Revelation 3:12).

Your old name was Lack—now it is Loved. Your old name was Shame—now it is Righteous. He bore the curse so you could wear the crown (Galatians 3:13; Isaiah 62:3). The tree that once looked like death became the Tree of Life. And in that sacred place of sacrifice, your new identity was born—not just forgiven, but forever named in His covenant, sealed in sacred blood, and led with divine loyalty.

So when you walk the paths of righteousness, you do not do so to earn His approval. You walk because you bear His name. The paths you tread become living testimonies of His character to the world. You are proof that grace transforms dust into royalty—and that the glory shining through the earthen vessel belongs entirely to Him.

The Beautiful Cost of Belonging

The cross was never only a payment for sin. It was a proposal—an invitation into eternal union. The Groom gave His life to name His Bride. He didn't simply save you from something; He brought you into something: His heart, His house, His family, His name.

"I in them, and You in Me... so that they may be brought to complete unity. Then the world will know that You sent Me and have loved them even as You have loved Me." — John 17:23

This is why He leads you. Not merely to correct behavior. Not merely to give direction. But to bring you home—to restore you to the intimacy for which you were made. The paths of righteousness are not roads of religious obligation; they are wedding aisles leading you into covenantal union.

The world will try to name you, defining you by failures, past, and pain. But Heaven has already spoken. Your identity is not up for negotiation. It was purchased at the highest price and sealed with the most sacred name. And now every step of obedience becomes more than movement; it becomes proclamation: *I belong. I am His. And He is leading me home—for His name's sake.*

The Crown of Thorns: The Mind of Christ Unleashed

When cruel fists forced thorns into the scalp of your Shepherd-King, they weren't merely mocking Him—they were unknowingly crowning Him (Matthew 27:29). The One who came to crush the curse at its root was now wearing its symbol upon His brow. Jagged thorns pierced deep, tearing flesh and sending scarlet down His face—rivers of mercy from the fountainhead of perfect love. What hell intended as humiliation, Heaven transformed into coronation.

The first battleground of sin was not hands or heart—it was the mind. In Eden, the serpent whispered lies that rewired humanity with shame, fear, and doubt. And so, in redemption, Jesus allowed the curse to touch the very place where torment began. The curse didn't merely bruise His head—He let it be broken open.

There, where accusation screamed, forgiveness sang a louder song. There, where confusion reigned, the mind of Christ (1 Corinthians 2:16) was forged in blood and painted in grace. Every drop that flowed from His head was holy, targeted, intentional—carrying power to break anxiety and confusion, silence shame's accusations, heal trauma buried in memory, and end the reign of torment and mental warfare.

He bled where you battle—for every battle you would ever face. He took the crown of chaos so you could wear the helmet of salvation (Ephesians 6:17). Where thorns once grew from cursed ground (Genesis 3:18), He bore them as a crown to reverse the curse and plant peace in your soul. Your mind, will, emotions, intellect, and subconscious were always meant for life—super-abundant life (John 10:10 TPT).

This is what it means to be led in paths of righteousness: not merely walking toward a new destination, but being transformed from the inside out. His blood did not only redeem your heart; it renews your mind. Now, because of Him, you think differently, feel differently, live differently. His thoughts become your inheritance (Philippians 2:5).

These are His righteous paths—not only roads beneath your feet, but living highways carved through thoughts, will, emotions, and desires. His leadership restores you to your truest identity, guiding you into a way of thinking that reflects His nature (Romans 12:2).

Paths of Righteousness: Rewiring the Mind with the Shepherd

The Hebrew word for paths in Psalm 23:3—**Maʿgāl**—means 'entrenched tracks, grooves worn by repeated movement.' It evokes well-worn trails: not chaotic wandering, but deliberate direction. And just as repeated steps etch grooves in the earth, repeated thoughts carve pathways in the landscape of your soul.

Every belief you rehearse, every reaction you repeat, every story you tell yourself becomes a path. Over time, those paths become habits, mindsets, even strongholds—fortresses of thought shaping how you interpret reality. Some protect you. Others imprison you. But all of them can be transformed.

"We demolish arguments and every pretension that sets itself up against the knowledge of God… and we take every thought captive to make it obedient to Christ." — 2 Corinthians 10:4–5

The Spirit invites you into what we might call neuroplastic grace—the miraculous capacity to tear down destructive mental highways and co-create new ones with Jesus. Just as Nehemiah rebuilt broken walls, the Holy Spirit rebuilds the infrastructure of your inner world—thought by thought, truth by truth, grace upon grace (John 1:16).

Co-Laboring with the Mind of Christ

"We have the mind of Christ." — 1 Corinthians 2:16

This is not a metaphor; it is a divine reality. The Greek word for mind—**Nous**—speaks of shared perception, divine consciousness, Heaven's blueprint for thought. To have the mind of Christ is to be invited into a new way of seeing, interpreting, and responding—a way that aligns with His heart and reflects His righteousness.

As you partner with the Spirit, old pathways that once carried fear, shame, and self-hatred begin to fade. New trails emerge as fear pathways are pruned, hope pathways strengthen, love circuits expand, and trauma loops are overwritten by truth. This isn't just poetic language—it's physiology redeemed. Joy doesn't only make you feel better; it reshapes the chemistry of your mind, affecting cortisol and the nervous system, retraining how you respond to storms. And all of this is part of the Shepherd's leading—paths of righteousness forming within you for His name's sake.

You were never meant to be shaped by fear; you were designed to be shaped by glory. Every time you choose forgiveness over bitterness, you carve a new path. Every time you choose gratitude instead of grumbling, that path strengthens. Every time you choose worship over worry, a trail of righteousness deepens.

"We all, with unveiled faces, beholding the glory of the Lord, are being transformed into His image from glory to glory." — 2 Corinthians 3:18

Think of your brain as the hardware being retrained to run the operating system of Heaven, while your mind is the interface that trains the brain through beholding Him. As you behold Him, you become like Him—not through striving, but through seeing. This is not behavior modification; it is divine metamorphosis. You are, quite literally, beholding your brain into becoming.

And the One leading you is not merely a shepherd—He is Righteousness Himself. He isn't only changing your destination; He is transforming your internal map. Every step is more than movement. It is metamorphosis.

New Pathways, New Realities

When the Shepherd leads, He does not simply change where you are going—He changes how you walk there. New paths begin forming in your mind and heart: peace instead of panic (Isaiah 26:3), trust instead of terror (Psalm 56:3–4), belonging instead of abandonment (John 14:18), hope instead of despair (Romans 15:13).

This is not self-help. This is divine renovation. You are not improving the old you; you are being transformed into the likeness of the One whose name you carry (Ephesians 4:24; 2 Corinthians 3:18). And this is why He leads you: not just to bring you home, but to make you whole on the journey—not merely to direct your steps, but to renew your nature as you walk.

Soul Activation

Follow Me

Imagine the Shepherd before you—eyes ablaze with love, yet gentle and near. His presence radiates peace, and His voice carries both strength and tenderness as He extends His hand toward you.

Behind Him, a radiant path shimmers—golden, holy, alive with joy. It is a path carved by love, paved with righteousness, and sealed with His name.

"Follow Me," He whispers. "There is no condemnation here. Only companionship." (Romans 8:1)

Take His hand. Step onto the path. Feel the weight of striving fall from your shoulders as His righteousness carries you. Let His Spirit empower your every step. Let His name define your thoughts. You are no longer walking in circles. You are walking in covenant.

You are walking home.

Journal Prompts

1. When I stumble or fall, what voices do I tend to listen to first — shame, fear, or my Shepherd's call to rise again? (Proverbs 24:16; Romans 8:1)

2. Are there places where I've let yesterday's failures shape my perspective — and how is His truth inviting me to see myself as He has always seen me? (2 Corinthians 5:17; Romans 8:28)

3. What old paths of thinking is my Shepherd inviting me to leave behind? (Ephesians 4:22–23; Romans 12:2)

4. What new paths of righteousness is He creating in me as I follow His leading? (Isaiah 43:19; Philippians 2:13)

5. What would it feel like to live as someone sealed by His name — walking as one marked by His covenant and favor? (Revelation 3:12; Ephesians 1:13)

6. What shifts in me when I remember that I already bear the King's name and belong fully to His family? (Romans 8:16–17; Galatians 4:6–7)

7. What strongholds or mental pathways is the Spirit calling me to tear down and rebuild with truth, partnering with the mind of Christ? (2 Corinthians 10:4–5; 1 Corinthians 2:16; 2 Corinthians 3:18)

Now Declaration

The Righteous Path of His Leading

I am led by the Shepherd of righteousness. My steps are ordered by love, not by fear. (Psalm 23:3, Romans 8:14)

I am the righteousness of God in Christ. I walk covered, clean, and crowned. (2 Corinthians 5:21)

I am sealed by His name and called by His goodness. The King has written His name on my soul. (Revelation 3:12)

I am no longer wandering — I am walking in purpose. His covenant leads me in paths of promise. (Proverbs 3:5–6)

I am not striving to be worthy — I am clothed in His grace. My identity is a gift, not an achievement. (Isaiah 61:10, Ephesians 2:8–9)

I am crowned with His mercy and filled with His Spirit. The mind of Christ is forming new thoughts in me. (1 Corinthians 2:16, Romans 12:2)

I am His workmanship. Every step I take carries the imprint of Heaven. (Ephesians 2:10)

I am living proof of divine favor. Righteousness surrounds me like a shield. (Psalm 5:12)

I am not the sum of my past — I am a carrier of His name. My story is being rewritten by glory. (Romans 8:16–17)

I am walking home with Him. I am not lost — I am found, loved, and led for His name's sake. (Luke 15:5–6, Psalm 23:3)

Final Reflection

Led for His Name's Sake

The Shepherd does not push — He leads.

Each step is sacred, not random but redeemed, woven into the path His love prepared before you arrived.

You are not lost — you are lovingly led.

You walk not to earn His favor, but to reveal His name with every step you take.

You walk by faith — steady, sure, and seen.

Grace is not earned — it's received, a robe of righteousness you already wear.

Each step becomes worship, a quiet echo of the One who walks before you.

He leads you through changing seasons with steady grace, not demanding perfection, but delighting in your trust — for His name's sake.

He leads me in paths of righteousness for His name's sake.

Chapter 7

Yea Though I Walk Through the Valley of the Shadow of Death I Will Fear No Evil

Psalm 23:4a

The Beauty of the Valley

We often picture valleys as dark, dangerous, and desolate—places to avoid or escape. But in the language of creation, valleys are anything but barren. They are wombs of life: places where rivers cut through rock, where soil gathers richness, where fruit grows sweeter than on the mountaintops.

In the natural world, valleys are places of abundance. Rich soil produces the sweetest fruit (Psalm 65:9–10). Rivers carve the land into life-giving paths (Isaiah 43:19). Green pastures hide between towering heights (Psalm 23:2). The land itself becomes a sanctuary of rushing waters and soaring songs (Psalm 84:6). The valley is not a wasteland; it is a garden in disguise—a place where roots run deep and life thrives beyond the reach of winds that batter the peaks.

And the "valley of the shadow of death" is no different when seen through Heaven's eyes (2 Corinthians 4:18). What the world labels as danger, God calls an invitation. What looks like desolation is often the very ground where intimacy, provision, and glory are revealed most deeply (Isaiah 41:10). The Shepherd does not lead you into the valley to destroy you; He leads you through it to transform you.

The Shadow and the Light

"I will fear no evil..."

The valley is real. The threats are real. The danger is real. But death itself? It is only a shadow (1 Corinthians 15:51–55).

A shadow is evidence of a greater reality—light. It cannot kill you (Psalm 118:17). It cannot devour you. It cannot separate you from the love of your Shepherd (Romans 8:38–39). The Hebrew word for shadow, **Tsel**, speaks of shade—something cast by a source of light. Shadows can appear large and intimidating, but they have no substance. The shadow of a lion cannot bite. The shadow of a sword cannot pierce. And the shadow of death cannot claim the one whose life is hidden in the Shepherd's hands (John 10:28–29).

You are not walking through darkness alone—you are walking with the Light of the World (John 8:12). And where His light abides, fear loses its voice. When you walk with Him, shadows shrink to their proper size: powerless silhouettes beneath the brilliance of His presence.

Emmanuel: God With Us

"...for You are with me." (Isaiah 7:14; Matthew 1:23)

The centerpiece of Psalm 23:4 is not the valley—it is Presence. The Shepherd's nearness is the difference between despair and deliverance.

The Hebrew name Emmanuel—**Immanu-El**—means *'God with us.'* It is not just a title; it is covenant reality. He is not a distant observer. He is your present companion, with you in the lowest valley and on the highest mountain.

This is not a God who visits occasionally. He walks in fire (Daniel 3:25). He whispers in caves (1 Kings 19:12). He weeps at graves (John 11:35). And He never leaves your side (Hebrews 13:5). *"I am with you always, even to the end of the age"* (Matthew 28:20).

You are not forsaken. You are not forgotten. You are held—by the God who is with you, for you, and within you. This is the heartbeat of the valley: Presence overpowers peril.

The Shadow of the Miracle Worker

Your Shepherd casts a shadow—but it is not the shadow of death. It is the shadow of glory, miracles, and presence. The Greek word: **Episkiazō (ἐπισκιάζω)** means to *'overshadow, to envelop, to radiate from above with divine power and protection.'* It is not mere shade; it is saturation—being surrounded by the active presence of God.

This overshadowing appears again and again in Scripture. Episkiazō came upon Mary (Luke 1:35), the creative overshadowing of the Spirit that brought Heaven to earth through her womb. Episkiazō enveloped

Jesus on the Mount of Transfiguration (Matthew 17:5) as the Father's voice thundered, *"This is My beloved Son."* Episkiazō moved through Peter's life until even his shadow became a conduit of healing (Acts 5:15). Episkiazō filled the tabernacle (Exodus 40:34–35), so weighty with glory that the priests could not stand.

This is the same glory that overshadows you. The valley may feel dark, but you are not shadowed by death—you are overshadowed by episkiazō, resurrection power. What looks like despair is often soil for miracles. What feels like dread is often the stage where glory manifests.

"The Spirit of Him who raised Jesus from the dead dwells in you..." — Romans 8:11

You do not merely walk through the valley; you walk with the very atmosphere of God resting upon you. He is not only beside you—He envelops you. Your valley becomes sacred ground not because it is easy, but because He is there. And where episkiazō is, miracles are born.

The Crucifixion: When Jesus Gave Up the Ghost

On the cross, Jesus cried, *"Father, into Your hands I commit My spirit"* (Luke 23:46), and with that He gave up the Ghost. He did not die as a victim—He surrendered as a conquering King. And in that moment, He released the Holy Spirit so you could be permanently overshadowed by the Spirit of God.

The earth responded as glory erupted. The veil was torn (Matthew 27:51). The ground shook and rocks split. Graves opened and the dead were raised, entering Jerusalem as witnesses of the goodness of God (Matthew 27:52–53). The Holy Spirit flooded everything that looked like death and turned it into resurrection life.

This is what happens in your valley too. Even in your worst moment, even in the deepest night, the same Spirit that raised Christ from the dead is overshadowing you (Romans 8:11). Maybe this is what Habakkuk meant: *"The earth will be filled with the knowledge of the glory of the Lord as the waters cover the sea"* (Habakkuk 2:14). Perhaps it is in the valley, not the mountaintop, where you come to know His glory most intimately.

Light in the Valley

Darkness can never comprehend the light—and it cannot conquer it either (John 1:5). You were not destined for confusion; you were designed for brilliance. Jesus said, *"Let your light so shine before men, that they may see your good works and glorify your Father in Heaven"* (Matthew 5:16). Isaiah echoed the same call: *"Arise, shine, for your light has come, and the glory of the Lord has risen upon you"* (Isaiah 60:1).

Light always illuminates the darkness it enters. The world's darkness cannot extinguish the light of Christ in you, because Christ in you is the hope of glory (Colossians 1:27). The darkness you face is not proof of His absence—it is the stage for His revelation. The Shepherd King floods you with light so you can see yourself as He does (Ephesians 1:18 TPT).

In the valley, the only shadow that overshadows you is not death—it is the shadow of glory. The shadow that follows you is evidence of the Light within you: the radiant presence of the Holy Spirit bringing healing, deliverance, and divine transformation. And in that light, the valley loses its power to intimidate.

The Valley Transfigures You

The valley was never meant to weaken you—it was meant to transfigure you. It redefines fear as a doorway to miracles. It teaches your soul to breathe deep and walk boldly. Here, courage is not the absence of fear; it is the presence of trust. Here, weakness is not failure; it is the womb of strength. Here, sorrow is not wasted; it becomes soil for comfort, peace, and joy.

You do not leave the valley merely stronger—you leave with **Godfidence,** the confidence forged only by walking with your Shepherd through the shadows. Confidence that He never left. Confidence that you are known. Confidence that beauty truly does rise from ashes (Isaiah 61:3). Confidence that you are never not overshadowed.

If you had never walked through the valley, you might never have discovered how close He truly is. You might not have seen miracles bloom from dust. You might not have tasted His goodness in the dark. But you did—and now even the valley has become sacred ground.

The Fire-Light: He Never Left

Picture yourself walking a lonely trail at night. The valley feels eerie. Shadows stretch long and sinister. Fear whispers, *You're alone. You won't make it. This is the end.*

But then, just ahead, you see it—a fire burning. And beside it, your Shepherd, smiling, waiting, radiating glory. He was there all along. He lit the fire before you arrived. He never left—and He never will (John 21:9).

That fire is your reminder: you are not walking toward safety—you are walking with safety. You are not walking toward light—you are walking with the Light of the World (John 8:12).

The Playfulness of Trust

What if the valley became a playground of trust? What if, instead of trembling, you danced through it like a child holding the Father's hand (Matthew 18:3)? What if the valley was the place God designed to birth your boldness?

Then the valley becomes the valley of overshadowing (Psalm 91:1), the valley of transfiguration (Matthew 17:2), the valley of resurrection (Colossians 3:1 TPT), the valley of Godfidence—the valley where shadows become stages for miracles.

And most of all, the valley becomes the place where you behold Him—not from afar, not through doctrine, but face to face, Fire-Light flickering across your soul.

Soul Activation

Play Under His Shadow

Picture yourself walking through a valley. The mountains rise around you, the river sings, and the grasses sway green and alive (Isaiah 55:12). A shadow covers you—but it is not fear. It is the overshadowing of your Shepherd King.

You feel the firelight of Emmanuel warming your chest. You feel His hand in yours (Isaiah 41:13). You hear His laugh—deep, joyful, fatherly. And He speaks:

Beloved, do not fear the valley. I am overshadowing you. I gave up the Ghost so you could be filled with My Spirit (Acts 2:2 TPT). *I go before you and walk beside you. This is not the end of you—this is the deepening of you. Watch what I resurrect here.*

Journal Prompts

1. Where have I believed the valley meant abandonment — and what is Jesus revealing to me about His nearness right here? (Psalm 139:7–10)

2. What miracles is the Holy Spirit growing in this valley that I may not have recognized yet? (Isaiah 61:3)

3. What does it mean for me to walk in Godfidence — the courage born from Presence — in this season? (Psalm 23:4; Romans 8:38–39)

4. What beauty is God unveiling through the ashes of this moment, and how is He turning sorrow into strength? (Isaiah 61:3; Psalm 30:11)

5. How is beholding Him in this valley reshaping the way I understand His love, His character, and His heart toward me? (John 8:12; Isaiah 41:10)

6. Where do I sense His overshadowing — His episkiazō — covering me with glory instead of fear? (Luke 1:35; Psalm 91:1)

7. What part of my identity is being strengthened, refined, or resurrected in the valley? (Romans 8:11; 2 Corinthians 4:17)

Now Declaration

The Revelation of the Valley and the Shadow of Glory

I am not afraid — I am overshadowed by glory. The valley does not define me; Presence does. (Psalm 23:4; Isaiah 41:10)

I am held by Emmanuel. God is with me, in me, and ahead of me. (Matthew 28:20; Hebrews 13:5)

I am filled with resurrection power. The same Spirit that raised Jesus lives in me — even here in the valley. (Romans 8:11)

I am walking with the Light of the World. No darkness can overcome the fire within me. (John 8:12; Matthew 5:14)

I am not abandoned — I am accompanied. My Shepherd leads me with peace, surrounds me with protection, and covers me in love. (Psalm 139:7–10; Psalm 91:1)

I am transfigured, not traumatized. The valley has become sacred ground where fear bows and beauty rises. (Isaiah 61:3)

I am marked by Godfidence. My boldness is born from walking with the Shepherd, not striving alone. (Romans 8:14)

I am a carrier of miracles. Testimonies are growing in this valley that will feed generations. (Psalm 126:5–6)

I am a child of light, lit from within. Shadows do not scare me — they are proof of the Light I carry. (Colossians 1:27; Isaiah 60:1)

I am transformed in the valley. What once felt like the end has become the beginning of glory. (2 Corinthians 4:17)

Final Reflection

Beautiful Valleys

The valley is not your enemy — it's the soil where trust takes root and courage blossoms.

It's where the rain of tears becomes water for new life.

When the Shepherd walks beside you, even shadows shimmer with purpose.

You are not walking to death — you are walking through it.

You are not being consumed — you are being cultivated.

The valley is not barren — it's nutrient-rich with grace, where faith grows deep and roots hold firm.

And the One who walks with you is not distant — He is Emmanuel, God with you.

Even here. Especially here..

Chapter 8

Thy Rod and Thy Staff, They Comfort Me
Psalm 23:4b

The Shepherd's Protection and Presence

"Thy rod and Thy staff, they comfort me." — Psalm 23:4

Every great shepherd walks with two companions, not ornaments but powerful extensions of the heart. The rod is a royal symbol of authority, defense, and governance (Proverbs 13:24). The staff is a slender instrument of guidance, connection, and deliverance (Exodus 4:2–3). Together they embody the Shepherd's nature. Together they whisper comfort. One declares, I will fight for you. The other promises, I will never leave you.

These are not weapons of fear; they are expressions of love. You are not beaten into obedience; you are led into inheritance (Romans 8:14). You are not coerced into submission; you are comforted into royalty (1 Peter 2:9). The rod and the staff are living proof that the Shepherd is present, attentive, and near.

The Rod: The Scepter of the Royal Shepherd

In Hebrew, the word for rod, shevet, means branch, scepter, or tribe. It carries the language of kingship and belonging (Genesis 49:10). In the hand of the Shepherd-King it speaks of covenant identity, royal authority, and protective covering.

You're not merely tolerated. You're truly seen and deeply loved. His name has become your name, and you belong to the tribe of your Shepherd-King.

When your heart begins to believe whose you are, something awakens deep within your soul. Trust begins to grow in places where fear once ruled. The slow and beautiful process of becoming who you truly are begins when you remember whose you are.

Yet if we're honest, there are moments when the soul forgets.

We begin carrying responsibilities we were never meant to carry. We try to hold everything together, protect ourselves, fix what is broken, and control what feels out of control. Somewhere along the journey we drift from human beings to human doings—striving, proving, and carrying burdens our Shepherd never asked us to carry.

Often this striving is not born from pride but from pain. Somewhere along the way our hearts learn that life wounds and promises break. Safety begins to feel fragile. So the soul quietly puts on armor: control, performance, and self-protection. We hope that if we try hard enough—to be good enough—we can keep ourselves from being hurt again.

Without even realizing it, we begin carrying responsibilities that were never ours to hold, slowly forgetting that we have a Shepherd who never asked us to be our own protector. He truly understands our frame (Psalm 103:14).

The Shepherd's authority is not harsh. It's protective, steady, and careful. He does not lead us with shame; He protects us from it. The soul; mind, will, emotions, and thoughts—sometimes try to convince us otherwise. The wounds of our past whisper loudly like an echo chamber of familiarity. Fear grips the inner world and disguises itself as protection when in reality it is the predatory voice of shame and pain.

What we truly need is the comfort of His love that drives away fear (Psalm 23:4, TPT).

These are the places our Shepherd steps in.

He drives back predators, crushes the power of the enemy, and establishes boundaries of safety around our lives. These burdens and wounds were things we were never meant to live with or carry. Slowly we place them back into His hands.

We begin to recognize that our strength comes from His shoulders, not our own.

This is His government—the authority that can whisper to chaos,

"Peace, be still." (Mark 4:39)

As Isaiah beautifully writes: "Perfect, absolute peace surrounds those whose imaginations are consumed with You; they confidently trust in You." — Isaiah 26:3 (TPT)

Something deeper happens as we yield to our Shepherd. We begin to see that He's been guarding, guiding, and protecting us all along. Every movement of His hand is shaping us into the royalty we were created to be (Revelation 1:6).

His authority and strength comfort our soul; they never constrict it. When we finally are able to relax and let go, we suddenly discover we're able to breathe again. Because the weight of the battle was never meant to rest on our shoulders.

"The government will rest on His shoulders." — Isaiah 9:6

So often our souls take on too much responsibility. We carry the weight of outcomes, relationships, wounds, expectations, and fears. Sometimes we care so deeply that we forget we are the ones being cared for.

This is where the Shepherd gently reminds us,

"Not by might nor by power, but by My Spirit." — Zechariah 4:6

We were never designed to live by our own authority or self-protecting strength. We were designed for trust and union.

"In that day you will know that I am in My Father, and you are in Me, and I am in you." — John 14:20

From this place His grace becomes more than enough for whatever we face (2 Corinthians 12:9). Trust begins to replace striving. Rest begins to quiet fear (Hebrews 4:9–11).

And when our thoughts wander like sheep without a shepherd (Matthew 9:36), we remember something deeply comforting.

He is here.

Always faithful.

Personally present.

Shepherd with you.

Sometimes the most spiritual thing we can do is stop striving and simply let Him carry what was never ours to hold.

"Cast all your cares upon Him, for He cares for you." — 1 Peter 5:7

Slowly and sometimes reluctantly, we hand over the false responsibilities our souls have been carrying. We place them into the hands of the One whose rod and staff guide us and compassionately soothe the deepest places of our hearts.

You were never meant to do life alone.

You were meant to be met by Him.

So breathe deeply.

Let the tension in your soul begin to release.

The Shepherd is here.

The burden is no longer yours to carry.

He prepares a place for you right now (John 14:2–3). You're not pushing through. You're not facing these battles alone. You're resting in the quiet confidence of the Ancient of Days (Daniel 7:22), whose faithful presence is the promise that never fails.

Take a moment and soak this in. You deserve this and He delights in you.

Discipline as Love, Not Shame

"Thy shevet... comforts me." — Psalm 23:4

To be a disciple is to be formed by love. Even the English word *discipline* shares a root with disciple—one who is teachable, moldable, entrusted with truth. In Hebrew, *shevet* carries this heart: authority that guides, protects, and lovingly shapes.

Hebrews 12 tells us God disciplines those He loves—not to punish, but to transform; not to control, but to conform you to the image of Christ. This is not conformity, it's the beauty of your originality. (Romans 8:29). The Shepherd's correction is not rejection; it is redirection. It is not condemnation; it is confirmation that you are His.

To follow Jesus is to whisper, teach me, Shepherd. Shape me. I trust You (Proverbs 3:5,6).

His discipline is proof of belonging. His correction is a covenant promise. You are not cast off—you are drawn near. You are not being punished—you're being prepared. The rod comforts because it means your Shepherd cares enough to mold you.

Molded for Glory

The hands that hold the shevet are the same hands that formed galaxies—and they are forming you. To be shaped by the Shepherd is not evidence of failure; it's the mark of favor. He molds those He loves, not to diminish them but to reveal them. He is the Potter, and you are the clay (Isaiah 64:8), and His shaping is never generic. It is intentional, personal, precise.

He knows the design He dreamed when He formed you (Psalm 139:14). He knows the purpose He planted in your soul before time began (Jeremiah 1:5). And with every press of His hand, He awakens the truest version of who you already are. His molding doesn't strip you—it reveals you. It doesn't control you—it completes you. It doesn't erase your personality—it refines it.

The glory doesn't depend on the vessel's perfection; it depends on the presence within (2 Corinthians 4:7). Fragile? Yes. Flawed? Often. But chosen, cherished, and filled with glory? Always.

Within you is hidden treasure: the Hebrew word for *delight* in Psalm 37:4 carries the sense of becoming soft, pliable, moldable. *"Delight yourself in the Lord, and He will give you the desires of your heart"* (Psalm 37:4). Do you see it? Delighting is yielding. Yielding is becoming moldable. And being moldable is the posture that allows Him to shape desire itself.

When you yield to His shaping, His desires become your desires. His dreams become your direction. His glory shines through places you once thought too broken to be beautiful. And as you delight in Him, something miraculous unfolds: you begin to discover that the desires of your heart are met above and beyond anything you could ask for or imagine (Ephesians 3:20).

Your surrender becomes the seed of fulfillment. Your yielding becomes the birthplace of dreams you never thought possible. He breathes life into the longings you entrust to Him, and they blossom into realities more radiant, more holy, and more aligned with Heaven's intention than anything your mind could have conceived.

Every crack becomes a window for His light. Every scar becomes a signpost of His mercy. What once disqualified you becomes the platform for His majesty. The rod of correction is shaping you for glory.

Bowing to Royalty

Every tribe and tongue will one day bow before the name of Jesus (Philippians 2:10–11). Some will bow under the weight of truth too great to resist (Revelation 6:15–17). But others—the beloved, the willing—will bow in awe, wonder, and love (Psalm 95:6).

Bowing is not humiliation; it is liberation. It is the posture of trust, the surrender of control. When you bow, you exchange anxiety for peace (Philippians 4:7). When you yield, you trade striving for serenity. When you submit, you step beneath the covering of His wisdom and strength.

And in that sacred posture, your perspective begins to shift—from dread to delight, from fear to faith, from survival to peace. This is what the rod accomplishes: not domination, but direction; not fear, but the discipline of comfort through love.

The Staff: Trust, Testimony, and Resurrection Power

If the rod declares, *I will fight for you*, the staff whispers, *I will walk with you*.

The staff is a symbol of guidance, dependence, and faithfulness. In the hands of a shepherd, it rescues wandering sheep from danger, draws the beloved close, and gently redirects those who stray. But it is more than a tool—it is a timeline of testimony.

Ancient shepherds often carved memories and miracles into their staffs—etched reminders of God's faithfulness, carried wherever they went (Deuteronomy 6:12). The staff was a story furnished by faithfulness, a history of hope held in the palm of the hand.

When God asked Moses, *"What is that in your hand?"* (Exodus 4:2), the answer revealed was more than a stick—it was a vessel of miracles. Moses lifted his staff and seas surrendered (Exodus 14:16). Elisha stretched forth a staff and death reversed (2 Kings 4:29–35). The staff became a living symbol of resurrection power.

Red Sea Moments: Remembering the Testimony

The valley often brings you face-to-face with impossible waters. When the way forward seems blocked and fear stands like a wall before you, reach for the staff of testimony. This is your Red Sea moment.

Moses—whose name means *"drawn out"*—was drawn from the water to part it. And so are you. The same Spirit who parted seas lives in you. The same power that split waters will make a way again (Romans 8:11)

"Stand still, and see the salvation (Yeshua) of the Lord." — Exodus 14:13

The Hebrew name **Yeshua**—salvation—is the name of Jesus. When you stand still, you are not waiting on an outcome; you are waiting with a

Person. And in that waiting, you will hear the Shepherd whisper, *I've done it before. I'll do it again.*

The testimony of Jesus is the spirit of prophecy (Revelation 19:10). What He did once becomes a promise of what He will do again. Suddenly the impossible parts. Fear is swallowed. Shame drowns. Trauma collapses under the weight of grace. And you walk through on dry ground—led by His staff, covered by His presence, washed in His blood (Isaiah 52:12).

Comfort in His Hands

The word comfort in Hebrew is: **Nacham**—'to console, to breathe deeply, to restore and revive.' That's what His rod and staff do: they breathe life back into you.

His rod comforts because He defends you (Exodus 14:14). His staff comforts because He lifts and leads you (Psalm 18:35). He knows the way (Psalm 32:8). You are not left wandering (Psalm 119:105). You are not left defenseless (Psalm 91:2).

You are led by a Shepherd who knows how to part seas, silence storms, and guide you home. This is why the psalmist said comfort—because every time the rod steadies or the staff draws near, it is love in motion. It is Presence reaching toward you. It is Heaven reminding you: **You are safe here.**

Soul Activation

Molded in the Valley

Be still and let the noise fade. The Shepherd is near.

You are not lost—you are led. You are not forsaken—you are being formed. This valley is not punishment; it is a place of shaping—not to diminish you, but to reveal you.

Picture Him beside you. In His right hand is the rod—authority and defense. It taps your shoulder not to strike, but to seal you as His own. In His left is the staff—gentle and guiding. It draws you near when fear whispers or distraction tugs at your soul.

Can you feel His nearness? He raises the rod in defense over your life. He extends the staff as an invitation to trust. He breathes comfort into the deepest places of your being.

Now breathe with Him. Let His discipline feel like delight, not rejection. Let His shaping feel like love, not control. Let His hands reveal the masterpiece He has always seen in you.

You were never meant to break in the valley. You were meant to become.

Journal Prompts

1. What "Red Sea" moment am I facing right now, and what past testimony is God asking me to remember and raise like a staff? (Deuteronomy 7:18–19; Exodus 14:13)

2. How is Jesus leading me through impossibility as Yeshua, my salvation — even when I can't yet see the way forward? (Isaiah 43:16–19; Romans 5:10)

3. What would it look like to live aligned with the spirit of prophecy — expecting Him to "do it again" in my story? (Revelation 19:10)

4. What thoughts or fears is the Shepherd inviting me to surrender in deeper trust, so His rod and staff can truly comfort me? (Proverbs 3:5–6; Psalm 23:4)

5. In what ways is God molding me right now, and how might that shaping align with His dreams and design for my life? (Isaiah 64:8; Romans 8:29)

6. Have I resisted His shaping? What would it look like to yield with delight instead of fear, trusting His hands on the clay of my heart? (Psalm 37:4; Jeremiah 18:6)

7. Where do I sense His comfort breathing life back into me — through His defense, His guidance, or His nearness in the valley? (Exodus 14:14; Psalm 18:35; Isaiah 30:21)

Now Declaration

Restoring Identity, Authority, and Royalty

I am sealed in belonging, rooted in His authority and chosen for royalty. (Psalm 23:4; 2 Corinthians 5:20)

I am led by Love — guided by trust, testimony, and resurrection power. (Exodus 14:16; 2 Kings 4:29–35)

I am comforted, not condemned. His discipline is my discipleship; His correction is my covering. (Hebrews 12:11)

I am alive with testimony. The miracles of yesterday prophesy the victories of tomorrow. (Revelation 19:10)

I am one who remembers. I do not forget what He has done — I lift the staff of faith and declare, "Do it again!" (Deuteronomy 6:12)

I am unafraid of Red Sea moments. I stand still and watch Yeshua make a way. (Exodus 14:13; Isaiah 43:16)

I am revived in His comfort. His defense surrounds me. His nearness steadies me. (Psalm 18:35; Isaiah 30:21)

I am no longer a slave to fear. I walk in the identity of the redeemed — washed in the blood and called by name. (Isaiah 43:1; Romans 8:15)

I am led, not lost. The Shepherd goes before me and guards behind me. (Isaiah 52:12; Psalm 91:2)

I walk in holy wonder, led by the Spirit. I carry the rod of remembrance, the staff of belonging, and the fire of fearless love. (Romans 8:14; Song of Songs 6:3)

I am clay in the Potter's hands — molded with purpose, shaped with intention, and formed for glory. (Isaiah 64:8; 2 Corinthians 4:7)

I delight in His shaping. His hands are not harsh — they are holy, and they are crafting something radiant in me. (Psalm 37:4; Romans 8:29)

I am not being controlled — I am being crowned. I am not being diminished — I am being revealed. I am molded for glory. (Proverbs 25:2; Colossians 1:27)

Final Reflection

The rod and staff are not relics of religion — they are instruments of relationship.

They do not wound — they heal.

They do not enslave — they set free.

They do not terrify — they comfort.

The Shepherd's hands that wield them are the same hands that formed you, the same hands that fight for you, and the same hands that hold you.

And when you feel their gentle touch — the unwavering authority of the rod and the tender pull of the staff — you will know, beyond every shadow of doubt:

You are not wandering.

You are not alone.

You are deeply loved — and forever comforted.

"Thy rod and Thy staff, they comfort me." —Psalm 23:4

Chapter 9

Thou Anointest My Head with Oil; My Cup Runneth Over

Psalm 23:5b

The Head Comes First

"*You anoint my head with oil...*"

Why the head? Because it carries holy gateways—portals designed for presence, not pressure. From here the heart gives direction, and life flows outward into thought, word, and action (Proverbs 4:23).

Here beliefs are shaped, identity is formed, and the mind is renewed (Romans 12:2).

But the Good Shepherd does not anoint us to think better alone.

He anoints the head so the mind may rest in rhythm with His heart.

Before thoughts can be renewed, the heart must be reborn (John 3:3). Before destiny can pour out, presence must pour in. He anoints the head first so that every thought, every imagination, every decision begins to move to the rhythm of His heartbeat.

This oil does not linger on the surface. It seeps into hidden places, soothing wounds, healing memories, rewriting stories. It is not simply a shift in thinking—it is renewal of your whole self. Where issues once flowed from brokenness, now they flow from belovedness. No longer driven by pain, you are carried by love. This isn't cosmetic change; it is holy saturation—head and heart united in the harmony of Heaven's design.

Every Sense Saturated

The anointing flows down, covering every sense and reclaiming every doorway of the soul (1 John 2:27). It touches your eyes so you see not only what is visible, but what is eternal (Matthew 13:16). *"The eyes of your understanding being enlightened..."* (Ephesians 1:18). The anointing gives vision—truth, beauty, and destiny revealed.

It touches your ears so you hear faith's frequency (Romans 10:17). *"My sheep hear My voice..."* (John 10:27). The anointing tunes your hearing until lies fall silent and the Shepherd's voice grows clear.

It awakens your discernment like fragrance in the air. Your nose was made to carry the aroma of Christ (2 Corinthians 2:15)—a knowing deeper than logic, a scent of what is real and holy.

And then it touches your mouth. When the oil kisses your lips, praise ignites (Psalm 71:8), and your words begin to carry weight. *"Is not My word like fire...and like a hammer that breaks the rock in pieces?"*

(Jeremiah 23:29). But His Word doesn't only shatter obstacles; it pierces hearts, surgically restoring what confusion fractured (Hebrews 4:12).

When you speak His Word, you are not echoing into emptiness. You are voicing what Heaven has authored—and Heaven watches to perform it (Jeremiah 1:12). Even angels lean in to respond: *"Bless the Lord, you His angels...who do His word, heeding the voice of His word"* (Psalm 103:20). Every rhema carries dunamis—a freshly spoken word clothed in miracle-working power (Luke 1:37).

So when the oil touches your lips, your speech no longer merely encourages; it releases life, and life abundantly (John 10:10). Your anointed mouth becomes a holy vessel—to sing, to decree, to echo Heaven into earth. Not only comfort, but chains broken. Not only songs, but revival carried on your breath.

From Thunder to Tender: Anointing the Head Leads to His Heart

John, the beloved disciple, was once called a Son of Thunder (Mark 3:17)—passionate, bold, zealous. His fire burned hot, but it was not yet refined by love. We often imagine John as "the apostle of love," but that wasn't always his story.

When a Samaritan village rejected Jesus, John and his brother James were so offended they asked, *"Lord, do You want us to command fire to come down from Heaven and consume them, just as Elijah did?"* (Luke 9:54). It's easy to label that moment impulsive, but underneath it were deeper wounds: rejection, insecurity, and a desire for justice. They wanted to defend Jesus, yes, but they also wanted their pain avenged. They even reached for Scripture to justify their fury, quoting Elijah's actions as if divine precedent could baptize their anger.

But Jesus turned and rebuked them: *"You do not know what manner of spirit you're of. For the Son of Man did not come to destroy men's lives but to save them"* (Luke 9:55-56). It was a moment of holy confrontation—a collision between passion and presence, zeal and truth. Jesus was showing them that the right verse with the wrong spirit still misses the heart of God. *"The letter kills, but the Spirit gives life"* (2 Corinthians 3:6).

This is what the anointing does. It takes zeal and baptizes it in love. It doesn't extinguish passion; it purifies it. It takes strength and shapes it into servanthood. It takes the cry for vengeance and transforms it into a cry for mercy (2 Peter 3:9).

Later, at the Last Supper, John laid his head—the seat of thoughts, reasoning, and identity—upon the chest of Jesus (John 13:23). In that sacred posture, his thoughts came into alignment with the heartbeat of Love Himself. John didn't lose his fire; he discovered its true source. He didn't forsake his thunder; he learned what Spirit he was of.

We were never called to silence our fire. We were called to let it burn from the altar of His heart. When the anointing rests upon you, your passion no longer burns to destroy—it burns to heal, restore, and release Heaven on earth.

From Senses to Service

Five senses. Five-fold ministry (Ephesians 4:11). The anointing is not only for encounter; it is for commissioning (Luke 4:18-19). He saturates your senses so your calling can overflow (2 Corinthians 1:21–22), not because you have arrived, but because you have said yes (Isaiah 6:8).

You are anointed. You are chosen. You are His (1 Peter 2:9).

Overflowing Cups and Carnal Lenses

"My cup overflows..."

He does not stop at just enough. He is the God of more than enough (Ephesians 3:20). Yet too often we choose the wrong cup. We sip survival, drink scarcity, and nurse fear, lack, and insecurity because we see through carnal lenses instead of faith's eyes (2 Corinthians 5:7).

But Jesus, your Shepherd King, still cries out: *"If anyone thirsts, let him come to Me and drink"* (John 7:37). There is a cup of inheritance, a cup of abundance, a cup of overflowing anointing—and it is yours (Psalm 16:5).

Fat with the Anointing: Dāšēn

Here the Hebrew takes us deeper. **Dāšēn** means: 'to be fat, luxuriant, saturated with richness and abundance.' To be made fat in the anointing is not gluttony—it is freedom. It is the Isaiah 61 exchange: ashes traded for beauty, mourning for oil, heaviness for praise.

This is the very anointing of Jesus, the Anointed One. Christ is not His last name; it means Messiah—the One saturated with oil. He carried the Spirit without measure (John 3:34), and now the same Spirit rests upon you.

The Holy Spirit performs the great exchange, taking what is thin, burned out, wasted, and ashen in your life and replacing it with a weighty, thick, glorious anointing. This anointing fattens you with joy. It enlarges you with peace. It thickens you with grace and favor—not as a burden of heaviness, but as a glorious abundance that stretches you to carry more of Him.

You are fat with freedom. Fat with favor. Fat with the same oil that marked Jesus as Messiah. This is the overflow David sang of—a cup that runs over not only to satisfy you, but to spill Heaven's abundance into the earth.

Drink from Overflow

Overflow looks different than comfort. It can look messy (Acts 2:13). It looks abundant (John 10:10). It looks miraculous (Mark 6:42). And it is not limited to finances or success—it is the success of the Cross. It is the presence of God spilling over your life, leaking glory into the world around you (John 7:38).

You were made for overflow—created to carry it (2 Corinthians 4:7), designed to release Heaven on earth (Matthew 10:8). The Shepherd anoints you not only for intimacy, but for impact (Isaiah 61:1–3).

Soul Activation

Be Saturated and Drink Deep

Let this ripple through your thoughts. See Him—your Shepherd King—standing before you with a flask of sacred oil (1 Samuel 16:13). Watch Him smile as He begins to pour.

Oil rushes over your head, and your mind shifts—renewed (Romans 12:2). Your eyes clear—healed to see (Mark 8:25).

Your ears awaken—lies fall silent (Isaiah 30:21). Your lips ignite—praise erupts (Psalm 34:1).

Then He places a cup in your hands—a golden cup brimming with living water, joy, and unstoppable love (John 4:14).

Listen as He whispers: *This is yours. Overflow is your inheritance.*

Drink deeply, beloved. Be saturated. And let it spill to the nations.

Journal Prompts

1. What area of my life is most in need of fresh anointing — a renewing, a reclaiming, a saturation of the Shepherd's oil? (Psalm 92:10; 1 John 2:27)

2. Where have I been drinking from survival, scarcity, or fear — and how is Jesus inviting me to drink from the overflowing cup of abundance? (John 10:10; John 7:37)

3. Which sense — sight, hearing, discernment, speech — needs to be reclaimed by the anointing so I can see, hear, smell, and speak with Heaven's clarity? (Ephesians 1:18; John 10:27)

4. What thoughts or memories need to come under the oil of renewal so they can be healed, rewritten, and aligned with the heartbeat of Jesus? (Romans 12:2; John 3:3)

5. Where do I see signs of overflow beginning — places where the Spirit is turning lack into abundance and thin places into dāšēn, saturated richness? (Psalm 23:5; Isaiah 61:3)

6. What would shift in my daily life if I truly lived as one already anointed — chosen, saturated, empowered, and sent? (1 John 2:20; Luke 4:18)

7. What cup have I been holding that needs to be exchanged for the Shepherd's overflowing cup of inheritance, joy, and presence? (Psalm 16:5; John 4:14)

Now Declaration

Anointing and Overflow

I am anointed — chosen, saturated, and set apart by God's hand and heart (1 John 2:20).

My mind is renewed, heart restored, thoughts covered with peace, and I live in overflow (Romans 12:2; John 14:27).

I live aligned with Heaven: not from trauma but from truth, not in fear but in love (2 Timothy 1:7).

I drink from abundance; I overflow with glory everywhere I go (John 7:38; Psalm 23:5).

The Spirit's oil abides, empowers, and transforms me daily (1 Samuel 16:13; Acts 1:8).

I am fat with the anointing — thick with joy, heavy with peace, saturated with grace (Isaiah 61:3; Proverbs 11:25).

I am commissioned: the anointing is not only intimacy — it is impact (Luke 4:18; Isaiah 61:1).

I release hope, healing, and miracles with the words of my mouth (Jeremiah 1:9; John 6:63).

I live in lavish grace — my cup runs over with joy, wisdom, peace, and purpose (Ephesians 3:20).

Final Reflection

Holy Spirit Encounter

Pause here.

Do not rush past this moment. For the One like a mighty rushing wind is here (Acts 2:2).

Everything you have read is more than revelation — it is invitation. It is oil waiting to be poured into your reality.

Take a minute. Breathe deeply. Let your spirit remember:

You are anointed — chosen, saturated, set apart.

Your head is covered — thoughts aligned with heaven's heartbeat.

Your senses are reclaimed — eyes enlightened, ears awakened, discernment sharpened, lips ignited.

You are fat with the anointing — carrying beauty for ashes, heavy glory instead of heaviness.

Your cup is overflowing — rivers of abundance ready to spill into the earth.

Now invite the Holy Spirit to make it real:

"Holy Spirit, come.

Saturate every part of me with Your oil.

I yield my thoughts, my senses, my words, and my desires.

Anoint my life afresh — from the top of my head to the soles of my feet.

Let the weight of Your glory rest on me.

Let the fragrance of Christ flow through me.

Let rivers of living water pour out of me to heal, restore, and awaken the world around me.

I receive Your anointing — not for a moment, but for a movement.

I am Yours — fully, completely, forever."

Now rest.

Be still and notice His presence — the warmth, the weight, the whisper.

This is not imagination.

This is encounter.

Stay as long as you need.

Let the oil keep flowing.

Let the overflow begin.

Chapter 10

Thou Preparest a Table Before Me in the Presence of Mine Enemies
Psalm 23:5a

The Table of the King

It should stop us in our tracks. The Shepherd doesn't only rescue us when we're lost. He doesn't only restore us when we're broken. He doesn't only lead us when we're weary. He hosts us (Luke 12:37). And not with rations or scraps—but with a feast.

"Thou preparest a table..."— Psalm 23:5

The Hebrew paints this picture vividly. He doesn't hand you a quick meal to get you by—He sets a banquet table, intentionally arranged, beautifully adorned, overflowing with love, belonging, and the aroma of victory (Psalm 36:8). And He does it right in the face of every enemy.

This is more than hospitality—this is honor. More than provision—this is proximity. More than comfort—this is covenant.

Shulchan: The Table of Reconciliation

In Hebrew, the word for table is **Shulchan**, from the root shul, meaning: 'to stretch out, to spread, or to send forth.' But it means far more than furniture—it speaks of a meal prepared with purpose, a space of invitation, a gathering ground for covenant.

In ancient times, if a family had no physical table, they would stretch out lambskins across the ground to form a sacred meal space. The lamb's skin itself became the "table"—a soft, extended surface where family, friends, and even strangers could sit, eat, and seal covenant promises (Exodus 24:9–11). This act was symbolic: *"I offer my life. I extend forgiveness. I welcome you as my equal."*

Now look to the Cross (John 19:30). Jesus—the Lamb of Glory—stretched out His body across the beams of Calvary, becoming the ultimate shulchan: the table, the meal, and the covenant all in one. His torn body became the sacred space where heaven meets humanity.

He is the Table (John 6:51). He is the Meal (1 Corinthians 11:24–25). He is the Feast of Forgiveness (Luke 22:19–20). The Cross was the moment the Shepherd spread the lambskin—His own flesh—across the ground of eternity and said, "Come, sit, eat, and belong."

And even now, the invitation stands: *"Behold, I stand at the door and knock…if anyone hears My voice and opens the door, I will come in and eat with him."* — Revelation 3:20

Love That Feasts in the Face of Enemies

"Thou preparest a table...in the presence of mine enemies." — Psalm 23:5

This is not a feast in secret. This is not a hidden meal behind closed doors. This is a banquet before watching eyes—even the eyes of every power that once tried to destroy you. Why? Because every enemy—sin, shame, accusation, fear, sickness, torment, poverty, despair, demons and satan—has been stripped and disarmed (Colossians 2:15).

They have no authority left. They must stand and watch while you feast.

The table is a public declaration of victory. It is Heaven's way of saying, *"This one belongs here."* It is the throne room turned dining room—a space where laughter replaces accusation and joy silences every lie that said you didn't belong (Zephaniah 3:17).

The Lamb who was slain has become the feast that never runs dry (Revelation 7:17). And every enemy is a powerless spectator to the celebration of grace.

But sometimes...the battlefield isn't around us—it's inside us.

Sometimes we are the ones who pull back our chair before we ever sit down. Sometimes it is not the voice of the enemy stopping us—but the whisper of unworthiness inside us.

Maybe it's shame that slips in quietly, like a shadow over the heart. Maybe it's anxiety—a mind racing through what-ifs and worst-case scenarios. Maybe it's depression—a heaviness that tries to convince you that showing up is too much and being seen is too vulnerable. Maybe it's isolation, echoing through the corridors of your thoughts: Nobody really sees me. Nobody truly understands.

Maybe tables were never safe places for you. Maybe connection was always questioned, belonging always fragile, trust always dangerous. Maybe you learned to eat alone. To survive alone. To be strong alone.

But your Shepherd knows. He never shames your story—He heals it. He never rushes your healing—He prepares your place.

"I go to prepare a place for you..." — John 14:2

He has seen the silent tears you tucked into your pillow in the dark. He has watched you hold yourself together when life tore things apart. He knows every memory that tried to steal your worth, every wound that whispered unwanted, every betrayal that taught you to guard your heart like a fortress.

And still—He prepares a seat with your name on it.

This table was not thrown together. It was crafted with you in mind—infused with the affection of a protective Father, and laced with the nurturing comfort of a tender Mother (Isaiah 66:13). Here, trauma-bonded chains break without effort. Here, grace warms the coldest corners of your heart until walls soften and love becomes the only language left.

Here, you do not anchor yourself—Love holds you first.

And He whispers: *You belong here. You are not too much and never not enough. Your presence delights Me. Let Me host you. Let Me heal you. Let*

Me restore you. I prepare a table not because you earned it, but because you are Mine.

At His table, disappointment dissolves into hope. Belonging settles into your bones. Questions fall silent as peace becomes your language. Security wraps around you like the warmth of a home you always longed for but never knew. Here—at the Shepherd's table—you receive your beloved birthright. Here, your heart remembers what your spirit has always known: you were made for communion, not survival; for relationship, not distance; for rest, not performance; for love, not fear.

Where the Table Beckons You

This is not a table of striving—it is a table of belonging. Not a place you fight to enter—but a place where Love carries you in. Pull up your chair. Breathe again. Taste grace. Let joy loosen every guarded place in you. Take a deep breath and allow all the tension to dissolve. Let Love rewrite your worth.

The Shepherd has set the table. Your enemies must watch—and you get to feast.

Welcome home. Your seat is ready.

But maybe you say, "I hear all of this…but you don't know what I've done."

Maybe your heart whispers, *"I betrayed Him. I failed Him. I walked away."* Perhaps your distance wasn't forced on you—you chose it.

Perhaps the ache isn't being rejected by God—but believing you rejected Him.

Yet here is the scandal of grace: Jesus prepared the table knowing every failure—and He still set your place. He didn't prepare a table for the version of you that "gets it right." He prepared a table for the you that wrestles, wanders, and returns trembling.

The table is not the reward of the faithful—it is the restoration of the fallen. Even those who feel like betrayers hear the same invitation: *"Come—there is still room."*

The Betrayer's Seat: The Scandal of Mercy

And then...there's Judas (John 13:26–27).

On the night He was betrayed, Jesus extended the most honored portion of the meal—bread dipped in oil—to the very one plotting His death. In that act was the whisper of Heaven: *"There's still time. Even now, you are invited."*

It was mercy's unceasing plea, even for the one whose kiss would wound Him. Grace's relentless pursuit did not recoil from betrayal but leaned in closer, offering love that refused to withdraw.

Love's open door stood before Judas—still extended, still waiting, still welcoming him home.

How many times have we been Judas? How many times have we betrayed love, withdrawn in shame, or warred against the very One who calls us home? And yet...the table still stands. The place is still set. The invitation still rings out.

"But God demonstrates His own love toward us, in that while we were still sinners, Christ died for us." — Romans 5:8

Even in betrayal, even in rebellion, even in the farthest distance—you were never uninvited.

Enemies in Our Own Minds

Sometimes the most vicious enemies aren't external. They're internal. They whisper: *"You don't belong. You've gone too far. You'll never be enough."* (John 8:44)

But the Shepherd's eyes burn with fire and tenderness (Revelation 1:14). He calls you by name (Isaiah 43:1). And He speaks a better word: *"Come. The table is ready. The feast is prepared. You were never forgotten. You were never uninvited. You are never not Mine."* — Jeremiah 31:3

Even when we were enemies in our own minds, Christ reconciled us to God through His death (Romans 5:10). The table is where those lies die. It's where striving ceases. It's where shame dissolves and belonging begins.

Lean in. Rest your head—your mind—on the chest of your Shepherd (John 13:25). Home is where His heart is, and at the table of grace, even your thoughts find their belonging in the rhythm of His heartbeat.

The Freedom of Forgiveness

The table is costly—not just because of the feast, but because of what it took to make a seat for you. Forgiveness was the price. Jesus didn't simply invite you—He forgave you into your place (Luke 23:34).

And now, He calls you to walk in that same forgiveness—not only as one who receives, but as one who releases (Ephesians 4:32). Forgiveness may feel unfair, yet it is the justice of Heaven (Colossians 3:13). It may look like surrender, but it is strength in its purest form. It doesn't excuse pain—it trades it for peace.

To forgive is to come into agreement with the Cross—to say, *"I will not carry what Jesus already carried."* (Matthew 6:14–15)

It breaks chains, silences accusation, and frees the soul from the torment of holding on. There can be no true feast where bitterness remains. Mercy and resentment cannot share the same table. Forgiveness is the fragrance that fills the banquet of grace.

Ask Him: *"Lord, who do I need to forgive so I can fully feast?"* Because the table is not only a place of abundance—it's a place of alignment. Forgiveness clears the heart for communion and makes space for joy, the very joy that was set before Him. For love of you, He endured the cross, despising the shame, so you could sit beside Him under the banner of love (Song of Songs 2:4; Hebrews 12:2).

Forgiving Yourself: The Unseen Seat

For many, the hardest person to forgive is the one staring back in the mirror. We replay our failures. We punish ourselves for what we did—or didn't do. We speak mercy over others but hold ourselves hostage.

But hear this clearly: the Shepherd didn't prepare a seat for your "ideal self." He prepared one for the real you—the you who still wrestles, still scars, still heals.

To withhold forgiveness from yourself is to disagree with the Cross. Jesus has already declared you clean (John 15:3). Already paid the price. Already shouted, *"It is finished!"* (John 19:30)

The table is not waiting for a better version of you. It's set for you now.

The Perfect Reflection of the Father

Some still wonder, *"But what if the Father sees me differently? What if He's still angry?"* But Scripture is clear: *"God was in Christ, reconciling the world to Himself..."* — 2 Corinthians 5:19

"The Son is the dazzling radiance of God's splendor, the exact expression of God's true nature—his mirror image!" — Hebrews 1:3 TPT

The Cross was not the Son convincing the Father to love you. It was the Father, Son, and Holy Spirit together, united in love, moving Heaven and earth to bring you home.

"If you've seen Me, you've seen the Father." — John 14:9

"I and the Father are one." — John 10:30

The Father's heart is the Shepherd's heart. The same wrath Jesus has against sin, shame, sickness, and death is the same wrath the Father has—not against you, but against anything that breaks intimacy or distorts identity.

From manger to cross, from tomb to throne, every act of Jesus is the Father's heart revealed. He has never turned away from you. He never will.

You are wanted. You are liked. You are loved. You are welcome. You are home.

John the Beloved: The Power of Communion

John was once a Son of Thunder (Mark 3:17)—zealous, bold, ready to defend what he loved with fire. But it wasn't strength that transformed him—it was communion. Not just another mission or miracle, but the table.

There, in the glow of covenant light, John experienced the nearness of Jesus unlike ever before. The One who had calmed storms was now kneeling as a servant, breaking bread with His friends, revealing that love's greatest strength is found in humility. The same hands that multiplied loaves were now giving Himself as the Bread. The same voice that commanded seas to be still now whispered, *"This is My body, broken for you."*

What John didn't yet realize was that this moment was more than a meal—it was a mirror. The table was preparing him for another table, one not covered in linen but in blood. The Lamb who served them would soon become the feast.

Jesus Himself was the Table. He was Communion Incarnate. He was Reconciliation made visible, love spread out in full surrender for the whole world.

And then came the Cross. The place where love is proven. The place where every motive, every allegiance, every theology, every heart is tested. As Martin Luther wrote, *Crux probat omnia—the Cross tests everything.*

It tests whether love is convenience or covenant, whether our zeal is self-driven or Spirit-led, whether our following is built on emotion or devotion.

When the test came, every man scattered—except one.

The Son of Thunder stayed. Tenderness kept him where fear could not.

John stood beneath the Table of the Cross, watching the Bread of Heaven broken and the Cup of Salvation poured out. He beheld reconciliation in its purest form: God, not counting men's sins against them, but absorbing them into Himself (2 Corinthians 5:19).

Every thunderous impulse within John was silenced—not by command, but by communion.

This is what the table does. It transforms the defender into the beloved. It turns reaction into reverence, and zeal into love. It makes us courageous enough to remain when everything in us wants to run.

Communion creates courageous vulnerability. The Cross reveals it.

For at the Table of Reconciliation, love doesn't just feed you—it remakes you.

And the same invitation still echoes to every son and daughter of thunder today: Beloved one—sit. Rest. Commune. Behold. Let tenderness become your strength. Let love rewrite your thunder. Let the table transform you.

Soul Activation

Return to the Table

A picture is worth a thousand words. Let your imagination take you to the place you've always belonged.

See the table—radiant and royal, set with gold and glory. The food is rich. The wine is alive (Isaiah 25:6). Your name is carved into the seat (Revelation 2:17).

Now see the Shepherd. His eyes are kind (Matthew 11:29). His robe is dipped in victory (Revelation 19:13). His hands—the same ones that stretched across the beams—are open, inviting.

He looks at you and says: *"You were never forgotten. You were never uninvited. This table was always for you. Feast, beloved. Forgive—even yourself. And let every enemy watch you eat in joy."*

Close your eyes, breathe deep, and linger in this for a moment.

Journal Prompts

1. What enemies in my mind have tried to convince me I don't belong at the table — and what thoughts need to bow to truth today? (2 Corinthians 10:5; John 8:44)

2. What part of my story still tightens when I imagine Jesus pulling out a chair for me and saying my name — and how might His love meet me right there? (Psalm 23:5; Isaiah 43:1)

3. How does Jesus extending the honored piece of bread to Judas reshape the way I think He responds to my own failures and betrayals? (John 13:26–27; Romans 5:8)

4. Who is the Holy Spirit inviting me to forgive so I can fully feast — without bitterness sharing the table with me? (Colossians 3:13; Matthew 6:14–15)

5. In what ways have I withheld forgiveness from myself, and how is that disagreement with the Cross keeping me from enjoying the feast prepared for me? (Romans 8:1; John 19:30)

6. When I picture resting my head on Jesus' chest at the table, what fears, lies, or accusations begin to lose their power? (John 13:25; Zephaniah 3:17)

7. What would my life look and feel like if I truly believed I am already seated with Christ at the table of the King, fully welcomed and secure? (Ephesians 2:6; Psalm 23:5)

Now Declaration

The Table of Reconciliation and Victory.

I am seated at the Table of the King. I belong here — not because of what I've done, but because of who He is. (Ephesians 2:6)

I am fully known and fully welcomed. My Shepherd has prepared a place just for me. (Psalm 23:5)

I am a covenant heir, not an outsider. (1 Corinthians 11:24–25)

I am surrounded by victory. Every enemy must watch me feast in joyous peace. (Colossians 2:15)

I am not too broken, too late, or too far gone. I have a permanent seat at the feast of forgiveness. (Romans 5:8)

I am no longer at war in my mind. The voice of shame is silenced by the voice of love. (2 Corinthians 10:5)

I forgive much, because I have been forgiven much. I live in the freedom of forgiveness. (Luke 6:37; Matthew 6:12)

I forgive myself, because Jesus already has. I no longer punish what grace has redeemed. (Romans 8:1)

I am transformed by His presence. My mind is aligned with His heart. (John 13:25)

I am His — always and forever. Nothing can uninvite me to the table of belonging. (Jeremiah 31:3)

Final Reflection

The table is not just a place — it is a Person.

It is Jesus Himself — stretched out, poured out, and unveiled in love.

It is the center of covenant.

The scene of reconciliation.

The stage of victory.

And there, in the face of every enemy, the Shepherd does not call you to fight — He calls you to feast.

So come — sit — eat.

For this is the table where shame is silenced, enemies are exposed, hearts are healed, and love always wins.

"Thou preparest a table before me in the presence of mine enemies." — Psalm 23:5

Chapter 11

Surely Goodness and Mercy Shall Follow Me All The Days Of My Life

Psalm 23:6a

Surely—The Unbreakable Promise

"*Surely.*" It's more than a word—it's a covenant vow. It's not *"maybe,"* *"if I behave,"* or *"if I pray enough."* The Hebrew word **'akh** is emphatic and absolute. It means: '*truly, indeed, absolutely, without exception.*' David isn't expressing wishful thinking; he is anchoring himself in the unchanging nature of God.

Surely is the language of divine certainty—the echo of Isaiah 55:11: *"My word will not return void."* It is Heaven's way of saying, You can take this to the throne room. It will not be revoked (Numbers 23:19).

The Shepherd's heart is not to chase you down with punishment. He is not waiting for you to fail so He can correct you. He is chasing you with blessing (Psalm 103:17)—with goodness, with mercy, and with a relentless love that runs faster than your shame and rewrites every chapter you've tried to tear out (Romans 8:28).

What follows you is not a mood, a feeling, or a fleeting promise. It is two covenant companions with names: *Goodness and Mercy—Tov and Hesed*—and they are not walking behind you casually. They are pursuing you with purpose.

Goodness—The Delight and Declaration of the Shepherd

The word for goodness is **Tov**—the same word God sang over creation: *"And God saw that it was... Tov."* (Genesis 1:31)

Tov is not shallow niceness that shifts with the crowd. The world praises niceness when you mirror its image—but niceness is often a mask. *Kindness is covenantal.* Your Shepherd King is not "nice." He is *kind*—and His kindness is not sentimental or weak. It is strong enough to lead you to repentance (Romans 2:4), bold enough to reform the way you think (Romans 12:2 TPT), and gentle enough to woo your heart back to wholeness instead of manipulating your behavior.

Before there was sin, sorrow, or shame, there was Tov—goodness. Before the fall, there was blessing. And when God crafted humanity, He didn't stop at "good." He said Me'od Tov— *"very good"* (Genesis 1:31).

Me'od means: *'exceedingly, abundantly, overwhelmingly.'* It is as if God looked at you and declared, *"You are the crown of My creation. My delight in you is without restraint."*

You were born into blessing before you ever battled a curse (Ephesians 1:3). And in Jesus, that blessing has been eternally restored. He became the curse so that the blessing of Abraham could rest on you without interruption (Galatians 3:13–14).

This is why Jesus said, *"Bless those who curse you"* (Matthew 5:44): because blessing is the greater law. It overrides the curse (Romans 12:21), silences lies, resets atmospheres, and breaks generational cycles (Exodus 34:6–7).

If you created something *exceedingly, abundantly good,* you would protect it, pursue it, and pour your best into it. That's exactly what the Shepherd does.

Goodness and Mercy That Follows

He pursues you with the two greatest expressions of His covenant—goodness and mercy. His goodness doesn't just rest on you; it follows you, even into your wandering (Psalm 65:11). It sweeps up your messes. It redeems your missteps. It leaves beauty in the wake of brokenness (Isaiah 61:3).

Once His blessing rests on you, no curse can outlast it, outrun it, or override it. It is the steady current of His love, always flowing toward you.

Mercy—The Covenant Pursuit—Chesed

The Hebrew word for mercy is **Chesed**—a word so rich that no single English word can contain it. It is steadfast love (Jeremiah 31:3). It is *covenant faithfulness* (Lamentations 3:22–23). It is *loyal devotion that will never let go* (Hosea 2:19–20).

Chesed is not a mood—it is a marriage. It is not based on your performance—it is anchored in God's nature (Psalm 136:1). It says: *"Even when you run, I will pursue you. Even when you fall, I will pick you up. Even when you forget Me, I will never forget you."* (Isaiah 49:15–16)

If **Ahavah** is love felt and **Chen** is grace given, Hesed is love plus grace plus loyalty braided into unstoppable action—bending low to carry, staying when others leave, rebuilding what was broken, providing what was squandered.

Allegory of Chesed

Imagine a shoreline at sunset—gold and rose brushed across the sky. You stand barefoot, unsure you belong. Your mistakes echo like waves. From the horizon, a tide begins to rise—not wild, but steady. A pursuit that will not turn back. Each time it reaches you, it leaves gifts: shells of beauty, pearls from the deep, stones etched with promises.

This is Chesed. It comes for you when you run. It wraps you when you fall. It carries the warmth of the Shepherd's gaze and the weight of His delight. No matter how many times you push it away, it returns—*unoffended, unwavering, unstoppable*—until your heart turns homeward.

It is not here to judge you. It is here to love you back to life.

Chesed Is Scandalous

Jonah couldn't stomach it when Nineveh repented (Jonah 4:2). The older brother resented it when the prodigal returned (Luke 15:28–32).

Religion hates it because it isn't "fair." But Chesed doesn't operate by fairness—it operates by covenant.

Picture a shepherd rescuing a lamb tangled in thorns, dressing its wounds, and carrying it home—only for that lamb to run away again. The shepherd doesn't sigh or scold. He runs after it with the same joy every time.

That is Chesed—covenant love with no exit strategy.

The Glory Graffiti

When goodness and mercy follow you, they leave a mark—not of shame, but of glory. God paints over the gray walls of your past with the colors of His covenant. It is holy street art spelling three words only Heaven can write: *Forgiven. Loved. Mine.*

The enemy calls it vandalism. Heaven calls it evidence. And when people pass by your story, they stop and stare—because they see what God can do with a surrendered canvas.

This is why we surrender to His Chesed: it restores identity. It breaks off every counterfeit the world parades as "diversity," leaving the soul empty and disoriented (Isaiah 43:19).

Your true identity is seamless, priceless, glorious, and complete in Him. It is formed by the One who knows you deeply and loves you extravagantly. He seals you with covenant love (Chesed), securing your belonging—and you awaken new (John 3:3; 2 Corinthians 5:17): *born again, new creation, true identity.*

Shall Follow Me

The Hebrew word for follow is **Radaf**—'to pursue, chase down, hunt with determination.' It is not passive—it is relentless. It is the same word used for armies pursuing until the mission is complete.

Goodness (Tov, Me'od Tov) and Mercy (Chesed) do not trail behind hoping to catch up. They hunt you down with covenant ferocity.

All the Days of My Life

This pursuit isn't seasonal. It doesn't hinge on your faith level, mood, or behavior. It is an all-the-days, no-days-off covenant.

Blessing is still the greater law. Mercy is still the stronger reality. And both pursue you until your final breath here and your first breath in eternity.

Blessing in Your Wake

What kind of Shepherd leads like this? The One who blesses before you arrive (Deuteronomy 28:2), orders your steps (Psalm 37:23), claims territory for you (Deuteronomy 11:24), and redeems wasted places (Joel 2:25).

You leave blessing footprints (Isaiah 52:7), mercy footnotes (Psalm 103:4), and goodness graffiti over failures you thought disqualified you (Romans 8:1). He doesn't erase your story—He rewrites it in glory (Isaiah 61:7).

The Overflowing Yes

Let this thunder in your spirit:

"No matter how many promises God has made, they are 'Yes' in Christ. And through Him the 'Amen' is spoken by us to the glory of God." — 2 Corinthians 1:20

All means:

Healing is yours (Isaiah 53:5).

Peace is yours (John 14:27).

Provision is yours (Philippians 4:19).

Wisdom is yours (James 1:5).

Inheritance is yours (Ephesians 1:11).

You do not live on grace's leftovers. You live in its overflow (Romans 8:32).

Soul Activation

Turn Around and See

Let this dwell within you until the scene comes alive. Picture yourself walking forward—bold, free, joyful. Now turn around. What do you see?

Goodness (Tov, Me'od Tov).

Mercy (Chesed).

Pursuit (Radaf).

They are not behind you shaking their heads. They are dancing in your dust, collecting broken pieces, turning them into bouquets of grace (Isaiah 61:3).

And you hear your Shepherd whisper: *Surely... surely...I will never stop pursuing you with My love. You are Mine. Forever and always, I chase you with blessing.* (Jeremiah 31:3)

Journal Prompts

1. Where have I mistaken God's kindness (tov) for niceness — and how is He inviting me into a deeper revelation of His covenant goodness? (Psalm 33:5; Romans 2:4)

2. In what areas of my life have I assumed I'm being "chased" by consequences, when Scripture says I'm being pursued (radaf) by blessing? (Psalm 23:6; Deuteronomy 28:2)

3. Where has chesed — God's steadfast, covenant love — already rewritten chapters I thought were beyond repair? (Lamentations 3:22–23; Psalm 103:4)

4. What story from my past still feels unfinished… and what would it look like to invite chesed to finish it with glory instead of guilt? (Isaiah 61:3; Joel 2:25)

5. How have I defined myself by failure instead of favor — and what new name does the Shepherd want to speak over me today? (Isaiah 62:2; Matthew 3:17)

6. What would change in my daily life if I truly believed that blessing, not punishment, is the greater law over me? (James 2:13; Galatians 5:23)

7. Where do I sense goodness and mercy dancing in my dust — turning the broken pieces into bouquets of grace? (Psalm 65:11; Romans 8:28)

Now Declaration

The Promise of Pursuing Goodness and Mercy

I am relentlessly pursued (radaf) by goodness and mercy. (Psalm 23:6)

I am surrounded by chesed — God's steadfast, covenant love. (Lamentations 3:22–23)

I am marked by me'od tov — the exceedingly abundant blessing of Heaven. (Genesis 1:31)

I am followed by favor, not failure. (Psalm 5:12)

I am a living testimony of redemption's grace. (Romans 8:28)

I am not defined by my past — I am rewritten by His glory. (Isaiah 61:7)

I am walking in the inheritance already given to me. (Ephesians 1:11)

I am a carrier of blessing, leaving footprints of beauty everywhere I go. (Isaiah 52:7)

I am confident in the certainty of His promises — every "Yes" is mine in Christ. (2 Corinthians 1:20)

I am pursued by love, empowered by grace, and established in favor. (Jeremiah 31:3; Romans 8:32)

Final Reflection

Abounding Relentless Pursuing Love

Pause here. Don't rush ahead. Let everything you've just read — every truth about goodness, mercy, pursuit, and covenant — move from your head into your heart.

See the Shepherd standing before you — eyes burning with joy, hands extended in welcome. Hear His voice calling your name, not with disappointment but with delight.

This is the One who never stopped chasing you.

This is the One whose chesed has no exit strategy.

This is the One who calls you home — not as a servant trying to earn favor, but as a son or daughter who already belongs.

Whisper this prayer aloud:

"Holy Spirit, come.

Let the truth of who You are and who I am sink deep into me.

I turn from the false names and labels I've carried — shame, failure, orphan, outsider — and I receive the name Heaven calls me: beloved, chosen, and known.

Pursue every corner of my heart with Your chesed. Chase down every lie with tov. Rewrite my story with covenant love.

I surrender to being fully found. I choose to live as who I truly am — a child of the King, a carrier of blessing, and a vessel of mercy.

Let goodness and mercy not only follow me — let them flow through me, transforming the world around me."

Now, wait. Let His presence rest on you — weighty and kind.

In the stillness, feel His delight. Hear His whisper over you:

"You are Mine. You have always been Mine. And I will never stop pursuing you — not until you see yourself the way I see you."

Stay here as long as you need.

This is not information. This is identity.

This is home.

Chapter 12

And I Will Dwell in the House of the Lord Forever
Psalm 23:6b

Better Is One Day—The Beauty of Dwelling

"*Better is one day in Your courts than a thousand elsewhere...*" — Psalm 84:10

To dwell in the house of the Lord is not merely to exist near Him—it is to abide within Him. It is to breathe in abundance, to feast on love beyond comprehension, and to live in the atmosphere of divine extravagance (John 10:10). Even the servants in His house are treated with more dignity, joy, and provision than kings and billionaires in palaces of their own making (Psalm 84:4).

Who can fathom His goodness?

Who can measure the wealth of His kindness or the depth of His delight? (Ephesians 3:19)

This is what David was reaching for—the wonder of simply being home in God.

What It Means to Dwell

The Hebrew word for *dwell* is **yashab**—a word rich with intimacy and permanence. It means: 'to sit down, to remain, to settle in, even to marry.' Yashab is not about visiting. It is not a short stay or a seasonal arrangement. It is about belonging—about resting, rooting, and remaining (Psalm 91:1).

It is the image of a heart fully at home—not striving to stay, not afraid of being asked to leave, but settled in the knowing that it belongs. It is learning to rest in the reality that His heart has already made a home inside you (John 14:23).

Home Is Where the Heart Is

Home is more than a place—it is a presence. It is where you are known, safe, and free to let down every guard. It is where you can laugh loud, cry messy, sing off-key, and still be celebrated—not merely tolerated (Zephaniah 3:17).

Home is presence (Psalm 16:11).

Home is connection (John 15:4–5).

Home is belonging (Ephesians 2:19).

Home is union (Ephesians 1:11).

Every glimpse you've ever had—that worship moment that left you undone, that dream that wrapped your heart in wonder, that blessing that caught you off guard—was not random. It was a whisper of Home

(Revelation 21:3). Each one was the Shepherd calling you deeper into what has always been yours (John 10:3–4).

The Prodigal Son and the Elder Brother—Two Ways to Be Lost

It is possible to dwell in the house and still feel like a stranger. It is possible to feast at the table and still think like a slave (Luke 15:17).

The prodigal son was not only reckless—he was blinded by discontent. Surrounded by abundance, he fixated on what he believed was missing. His heart chased empty promises, fueled by insecurity and entitlement. He didn't leave because he lacked—he left because he lost sight of what he already had.

He wandered not only with his feet but with his thoughts, meditating on what he could do rather than resting in who he already was. This is the tragedy of an orphan spirit—you can live in the Father's house and still feel like you don't belong.

But the Father never stopped watching.

He never stopped calling.

He never stopped loving him home (Jeremiah 31:3).

When the son returned, rehearsing a speech soaked in shame, love interrupted him mid-sentence. The Father ran—not away from his mess, but into it. He kissed his dirty neck, wrapped him in compassion, and restored him completely. The robe redeemed his past. The ring restored his authority. The feast reawakened his identity.

Home was never lost—only forgotten.

Love never withdrew—it waited.

The elder brother, meanwhile, never left the property, yet his heart drifted far from presence. Like a sheep still in the pasture but deaf to the Shepherd's voice, he worked faithfully but lived disconnected, trying to earn what was already his. He saw himself as a laborer, not a beloved son. His service was loyal, but his heart was heavy with resentment. He stood near the house but refused to enter its joy.

Psalm 23 shows us the Shepherd preparing a table in the presence of enemies. Luke 15 shows us the Father preparing a feast in the presence of family. Yet the elder brother would not join—not because he wasn't invited, but because grace offended him.

The Father still stepped outside—not to condemn, but to invite him back into joy (Luke 15:31–32). The prodigal had to come to the end of himself to receive mercy. The elder brother had to lay down his pride to experience grace. One ran and was met with compassion. The other stayed and was met with invitation.

Neither was disqualified.

Both were pursued.

Because the Shepherd does not merely recover what was lost—He restores what was broken.

Forever Means Forever

"Forever" is not poetic exaggeration—it is covenant language (John 14:2–3).

Forever means no eviction notices (John 6:37).

No change of address (Revelation 3:12).

No end to love (Psalm 136:1).

No expiration on favor (Isaiah 54:10).

No closing of the door to Home (Isaiah 32:18).

Home with the Shepherd is not a season. It is perpetual presence (Psalm 61:4). It is an eternal embrace (Isaiah 40:11). It is everlasting belonging (Psalm 27:4). It is a breath of fresh air that never fades, a place of rest that never closes, and a feast that never runs dry (Isaiah 55:1–2).

Soul Activation

Rest, Settle, and Belong

Let the eyes of your understanding soak this in.

See a house—not made of stone or wood, but woven of light, laughter, and love (John 14:2). This is your Father's house. This is the Shepherd's home.

You are not a guest.

You are family (Romans 8:16–17).

Hear the Shepherd whisper, *"Welcome home, beloved. Not just today. Not just until you behave better. Forever. You are Mine, and I am Yours."* (Jeremiah 31:3)

Now exhale.

Settle.

Dwell.

You are already Home.

Journal Prompts

1. Where have I lived like a visitor in God's presence when I was invited to dwell as family? (Psalm 27:4; John 15:4)

2. What abundance is already surrounding me that I've overlooked because I've focused on what I think is missing? (Psalm 23:1)

3. Where have my thoughts wandered — imagining life somewhere else, something else, or someone else — instead of resting in who I already am? (Luke 15:12–13)

4. What lies have promised me more "out there" than what the Father has already given "right here"? (Ephesians 1:3)

5. In what areas have I responded like the younger brother — running to self-reliance, escape, or striving? (Luke 15:17–20)

6. In what areas have I responded like the elder brother — resentful, withholding joy, or trying to earn what is already mine? (Luke 15:28–31)

7. What would it look like today to reenter the feast — not by performance, but by trust, surrender, and belonging? (Luke 15:22–24)

Now Declaration

The Covenant of Belonging

I am forever at Home in the heart of my Shepherd.

I dwell in His presence — not as a servant earning entry, but as a child fully embraced.

I am not a runaway lost in rebellion. I am not a striver stuck in resentment. I am the one He rejoices over — the one He carried, clothed, and crowned (Luke 15:20–22; Psalm 23:6).

I dwell, because I am loved. I stay, because I am safe. I feast, because I am family.

The Shepherd's joy is my strength, and His invitation is always open.

My soul is settled, my identity sealed, and my belonging eternal (Ephesians 2:19; Zephaniah 3:17; Revelation 3:12).

I am not on probation — I am in permanent covenant.

Forever means forever.

I am Home, and I am His.

Final Reflection

The Home Within

Every longing you've ever carried wasn't for a place — it was for a Person — Jesus.

Every quiet yearning for belonging has been the echo of Eden still alive within you.

From the beginning, the Shepherd never meant for you to visit His presence — but to live there.

You were made to dwell, not to drift. To rest, not to run. To belong, not to beg.

His house is not a distant promise — it's the atmosphere of your new life in Christ.

Behold, all things are new — you are His dwelling place now, and your heart beats in rhythm with His. (2 Corinthians 5:17)

The invitation is simple: Come home and stay. You are not a guest — you are family.

Not waiting for forever — already living in it.

You are Home.

Chapter 13

From Bummer to Glory: The Story of the Shepherd's Love
Closing Thoughts

From Bummer Lambs to Glory to Glory

In every flock, there are bummer lambs—the ones rejected by their mothers, left without nurture or care. To the world, they are forgotten. To the flock, they are forsaken. But to the Shepherd, they are precious (Luke 15:4–6).

When no one else wants them, He bends low and gathers them into His arms. He holds them close, warming their trembling bodies against His chest. He feeds them by hand, sustains them through sleepless nights, and becomes their comfort, their provider, and their protector (Isaiah 40:11; Psalm 23:1–2). They learn the rhythm of His heartbeat before they ever learn to walk. They recognize His voice before they hear the bleating of the flock (John 10:3–4).

And when the bummer lamb is finally reintroduced into the pasture, something miraculous happens. It is always the first to run when the

Shepherd calls. It knows the voice that rescued it. It remembers the hands that carried it. It trusts the One who never let go.

We Were All Bummer Lambs Once

Every one of us was a bummer lamb—rejected, wounded, and alone (Ephesians 2:12). We wandered, searching for belonging, desperate for love. But the Good Shepherd came searching for us.

He found us.

He lifted us.

He held us (Psalm 18:35).

He healed us (Psalm 147:3).

And He brought us home—not as servants, but as sons and daughters (Romans 8:15–17).

Adoption—The Forever Seal

In the ancient world, adoption was more than acceptance—it was permanence. A biological child could be disowned, but an adopted child could never be cast away. Adoption sealed a person with irrevocable rights: full status, full inheritance, full authority, as though born of royal blood (Galatians 4:7).

This is why Paul writes:

"And you did not receive the 'spirit of religious duty,' leading you back into the fear of never being good enough. But you have received the Spirit of full

acceptance, enfolding you into the family of God. And you will never feel orphaned, for as He rises up within us, our spirits join Him in saying the words of tender affection, 'Beloved Father!'

For the Holy Spirit makes God's fatherhood real to us as He whispers into our innermost being, 'You are God's beloved child!'

And since we are His true children, we qualify to share all His treasures, for indeed, we are heirs of God Himself. And since we are joined to Christ, we also inherit all that He is and all that He has. We will experience being co-glorified with Him provided that we accept His sufferings as our own." (Romans 8:15–17 TPT)

This is your story.

You were not merely added into God's family—you were enthroned into it (Ephesians 2:6). You were not simply accepted (Ephesians 1:6). You are celebrated (Zephaniah 3:17). You are not merely included. You are cherished. You are chosen, sealed, crowned, and called His own—a royal heir, a beloved child, a priceless treasure (Isaiah 62:3).

From Bummer to Glory

We do not move from heartbreak to heartbreak. We do not go from rejection to rejection. We do not live as wounded lambs hiding in the shadows of our past.

We go from glory to glory (2 Corinthians 3:18).

Because we are held by the hands that will never release us (John 10:28). Because we belong to a Shepherd whose love cannot fail. Our souls are restored (Psalm 23:3). Our spirits are lifted (Romans 8:11). Our bodies are embraced as temples of His presence (1 Corinthians 6:19). Our inheritance is sealed (Ephesians 1:13–14).

We are not barely part of the family.

We are family.

We are not simply near the Shepherd.

We belong to Him.

We are no longer bummer lambs.

We are glory lambs—carried by His hands, crowned by His love, and transformed by His grace.

Chapter 14
The Fold Restores What Isolation Steals
Bonus Chapter

When Pulling Away Feels Safer

"And other sheep I have which are not of this fold; them also I must bring, and they will hear My voice; and there will be one flock and one shepherd." — John 10:16 NKJV

There are moments when pulling away feels like the only option. Maybe the people who were supposed to love you didn't. Maybe community became a source of pain instead of healing. Maybe you've convinced yourself it's easier to go it alone.

But here's the truth. *Isolation is not the same as rest.* And it is certainly not the same as healing.

Isolation slowly starves the soul of what it most needs—connection, safety, and shared strength. It lures you with the illusion of protection while quietly leaving you vulnerable to lies, discouragement, and spiritual attack.

"Whoever isolates himself seeks his own desire; he breaks out against all sound judgment." — Proverbs 18:1

The enemy loves to target isolated sheep. Not because you are weak—but because you are alone.

Solitude and Isolation Are Not the Same

There is a holy difference between solitude and isolation.

Solitude is when the Shepherd draws you away for stillness, intimacy, and strengthening. It is chosen, purposeful, and rooted in connection (Luke 5:16). Even in solitude, you remain anchored in identity, covered by community, and close to the Shepherd's heart.

Isolation, however, is when pain, fear, or shame push you away from others and from truth. It convinces you that hiding is safer, when in reality it leaves you more exposed than ever.

Jesus withdrew to be with the Father, yes—but He always returned. He came back to restore, to heal, to love, and to walk with His people. *Solitude strengthens your spirit. Isolation silences your hope.*

The Shepherd's Heart for the Fold

Psalm 23 is not the song of a lone sheep wandering far from the pasture. It is the declaration of one who has been led, fed, comforted, and restored within the safety of the fold.

The rod and the staff were never just for individual comfort. They were also used to guide the flock together, to pull wandering sheep back into safety, to protect against predators that hunt the isolated, and to continually remind every sheep, *You are not forgotten. You still belong.*

The Shepherd does not only want you healed. He wants you home.

Healing Does Not Happen in Hiding

You may have been hurt by people—including people in church. And that pain is real.

But hiding is not healing. And numbing is not restoration.

Sometimes the greatest breakthrough you are longing for is waiting in the very place you fear—connection with others. The right people will not be perfect. But they will be planted. They will be willing to sit with you, speak truth, encourage your heart, and gently call you back to life.

"Two are better than one... If either of them falls, one can help the other up."
— Ecclesiastes 4:9–10

The Shepherd often uses the fold—a group of messy, healing, growing people—as one of the primary pathways of restoration.

If You've Isolated, You're Not Alone

We all isolate at times. But you were never made to stay there.

You were made to belong. To be seen. To heal in the light. To grow in the company of others who are being led by the same Shepherd.

Let this be your gentle nudge. Come back to the fold. Not out of guilt. Not because someone expects it. But because your soul was never designed to thrive alone.

There is covering here.

There is healing here.

There is family here.

Soul Activation

Come Out of Hiding

Picture yourself standing on the edge of the flock, watching from a distance. You want to belong—but it feels risky. Then you feel it. The gentle pull of the staff. The comforting nearness of the Shepherd's presence.

You hear His voice—not in anger, but in love: *"You are still Mine. You have never stopped belonging."*

Now take one step closer. Then another. And watch as the fold opens wide—not to judge, but to welcome you home.

Journal Prompts

1. Where have pain, disappointment, or past wounds convinced me that isolation is safer than connection? (Proverbs 18:1)

2. How do I personally discern the difference between holy solitude that strengthens me and isolation that slowly drains me? (Luke 5:16)

3. What lies have I believed in moments of isolation — about myself, others, or God — that would not survive in healthy community? (Psalm 23:4)

4. When have I felt the Shepherd gently pulling me back into connection, even when my instinct was to withdraw? (John 10:16)

5. What part of "returning to the fold" feels hardest for me right now — and why? (Ecclesiastes 4:9–10)

6. Who are the safe, planted, healing-centered people God has placed in my life — and what step can I take toward connection with them? (Galatians 6:2)

7. What might my soul recover, receive, or rediscover if I allowed myself to belong again? (Psalm 68:6)

Now Declaration

The Power of Returning

I am not alone. I am part of the fold. I am loved by my Shepherd and covered in community. (John 10:14)

I no longer hide in isolation. I am drawn out of fear and into healing light. (Isaiah 42:16)

I choose truth over the lies of loneliness. My Shepherd has never left me. (Hebrews 13:5)

I embrace healthy community. I am surrounded by those walking toward restoration, just like me. (Psalm 68:6)

I come out of hiding. I return to the fold. I receive comfort, covering, and belonging. (Psalm 23:4, Ecclesiastes 4:10)

Final Reflection

Returning Is an Act of Courage

Pulling away may have felt like survival, but staying hidden was never the Shepherd's desire for you. The fold is not a place of perfection; it is a place of presence, where wounds are seen without being exploited, strength is shared, and healing unfolds through belonging rather than isolation. You were never meant to carry life alone, but to be known, covered, and restored among others who are also learning how to trust again.

The Shepherd does not shame the wandering sheep or demand explanations for the distance they've traveled. He calls them by name, meets them with gentleness, and leads them home. Returning is not a sign of weakness—it is an act of courage. It is the quiet decision to believe that love is still possible, that safety can be rebuilt, and that your story does not end in hiding.

The fold remains open, the Shepherd is still near, and you have never stopped belonging to Him.

Chapter 15

Final Encouragement: A Forever Invitation

Beloved one, Your journey is not over — it's just beginning.

As you step out from these pages, there is one truth you must not leave behind: your testimony carries prophetic power, for Scripture tells us that "the testimony of Jesus is the spirit of prophecy" (Revelation 19:10), meaning your story does not merely celebrate what God has done but actively releases what God desires to do again—your restoration becoming someone else's roadmap, your breakthrough becoming someone else's courage, and your healing becoming someone else's hope.

So if *He Restores My Soul* has awakened something in you—if the Shepherd has met you, healed you, spoken to you, or restored you in any way—I would be honored to hear your story, because your testimony will echo far beyond this moment, strengthening others for years to come and prophesying restoration into lives you may never meet; you can share your journey at **testimonies@luxorbispublishing.com**.

This is not the end of a book—it is the beginning of a lifestyle, a doorway into ongoing restoration, revelation, and radical intimacy with the Shepherd of your soul, because Psalm 23 was never meant to be read once and then shelved but lived as a continual invitation, an unending river, a homecoming that flows day after day. It is not merely poetry; it is prophecy. It is not simply comfort; it is your calling.

Return to these pages again and again—not to read them like a checklist but to sit with them like a love letter, to linger, to meditate, to revisit, and to receive (Proverbs 25:2), remembering that you are royalty and royalty never exhausts the riches of the King's house, for there is always more to uncover, deeper waters to enter, and another layer of glory waiting to be revealed. Each time you return, something new will open within you—your heart softening in new places, your eyes seeing more clearly, and your spirit hearing more intimately—as Heaven provides daily bread, fresh revelation, fresh comfort, and fresh strength, given day by day, word by word, breath by breath (Matthew 6:11; Matthew 4:4).

As the Shepherd restores your soul, the way you see yourself and the way you see the world will be transformed, your inner eyes enlightened and flooded with light as you begin to perceive the hope of your calling with increasing clarity and holy confidence (Ephesians 1:17–18; Isaiah 26:3), until what once overwhelmed you becomes the testimony you carry and what once named you bows before your true identity. Faith rises as His Word takes root (Romans 10:17), and the more you behold His heart, the clearer your identity becomes, because you come alive to who you are by knowing whose you are (3 John 1:2; Proverbs 23:7).

You are loved. You are chosen. You are royalty (1 Peter 2:9; Romans 8:16), and **nothing—no past failure, no present struggle, no future**

fear—has the power to separate you from His love, now or for all eternity (Romans 8:38–39).

So keep reading, keep receiving, keep declaring truth, and keep journaling your journey (Habakkuk 2:2), allowing Psalm 23 to become your soul's vocabulary—the meditation of your nights, the song of your days, and the restoration of your very being (Psalm 1:2)—and when life gets loud, hope feels thin, or joy seems distant, come back here, because Psalm 23 is not just a chapter; it is a heartbeat, the Shepherd's voice, and a forever invitation into love that cannot fail and goodness and mercy that will never stop pursuing you.

Blessings, union, and fire,

— Benjamin Straup

Chapter 16

Closing Prayers and Declarations

Final Journey Declaration

My Shepherd, My Home

Psalm 23; Romans 8:14; John 15:9; Ephesians 3:17–19

I am seen, known, and cherished by my Shepherd King.

I am not wandering—I am led by Love Himself, guided by His voice, and anchored in trust and joy.

I am familiar with His nearness, responsive to His tenderness, and confident in His strength as I follow where He leads.

I am living in continual abundance because my Shepherd provides without pressure and supplies without striving.

I am resting not because my work is finished, but because His work is complete, and His rest is my inheritance.

I am rooted in peace that resists fear and carries authority, because rest is not weakness and peace is my portion.

I am immersed in His delight, resting in radiant beauty as living waters restore my soul.

I am overshadowed by the Holy Spirit, who hovers over every place in me, birthing creativity, healing, and deep trust.

I am not a project—I am poetry, handcrafted with purpose and flourishing as a garden of grace.

I am walking radiant paths of purpose, clothed in righteousness, wrapped in royal identity, and crowned with joy.

I am renewed in my thinking as His Spirit rewrites my thoughts with glory and trains my mind in truth.

I am held by Love, not fear, and I live from a place where His nearness is my joy and His presence is my celebration.

I am safe in every valley because His presence turns shadowed places into sanctuaries.

I am comforted, championed, and protected by His rod of royalty and His staff of resurrection power.

I am held in His fierce affection, secured by His discipline, and strengthened by His faithful care.

I am seated at the Table of Belonging, dining not as a stranger but as family, welcomed as a cherished friend.

I am eating in peace, clothed in honor, and seated in victory beneath the banner of His love.

I am overflowing with fresh anointing as His oil restores what the world tried to empty.

I am alive to His Spirit, awakened in my senses, and attentive to wonder as every moment becomes an invitation into life.

I am followed—by goodness and mercy, which pursue me daily with covenant purpose.

I am looking back on my story and seeing wonders instead of wounds, revelation instead of regret, and redemption instead of ruin.

I am living a grace-soaked story where love has rewritten what life tried to destroy and restoration has the final word.

I am dwelling in His house, not as a visitor, but in the very chambers of His heart.

I am not traveling toward belonging—I am already home.

I am abiding.

I am overflowing.

I am delighted in.

I am no longer striving to be loved because I am already fully known and joyfully embraced.

I am hearing the Shepherd sing over me with delight, and I am responding with the symphony of my surrendered life.

I am living my story.

I am carried by my Shepherd.

I am singing my forever song.

I am sealed in the mighty, precious, ever-present, passionate, and powerful name of my Shepherd King—Jesus.

Final Prayer

The Shepherd's Seal

(Psalm 23:6, Isaiah 40:11, Romans 8:38–39)

Shepherd King,

You have led me into places I never dreamed I could walk (Isaiah 42:16). You have called me by name (Isaiah 43:1), healed my wounds (Psalm 147:3), restored my soul (Psalm 23:3), and anointed my life with Your unfailing love (Psalm 36:7–9).

I am Yours — fully, freely, forever (John 17:10).

I receive Your goodness (Psalm 31:19).

I surrender to Your mercy (Titus 3:5).

I walk in Your righteousness (Isaiah 61:3).

I feast at Your table (Revelation 19:9).

I drink from Your overflow (John 4:14).

I dwell in Your presence — today, tomorrow, and always (Psalm 27:4). Thank You, Shepherd of my soul, for leading me not just into green pastures, but into Your very heart (Ezekiel 34:14–15). Let my life forever sing: *"I am my Beloved's, and my Beloved is mine."* (Song of Songs 6:3)

I pray this in the precious name of our Shepherd King, Jesus.

Amen.

My Personal Favorite Version of Psalm 23
The Passion Translation

A Personal Tribute

We want to take a moment to honor two of the dearest souls in our lives, Dr. Brian and Candice Simmons, spiritual heroes and dear friends whose lives radiate the very beauty we long to grow into. Your journey reflects a rare and holy harmony, where childlike wonder is woven together with deep tenderness and an unquenchable passion for Jesus, and where kindness flows from you like a living river shaped by intimacy with the Shepherd King.

There is an awe you carry in every conversation, a nearness to Jesus that cannot be imitated and can only be cultivated through true union, and it causes your lives to shine brighter with every passing day—not because the path has been free of hardship, but because you have learned how to feast on joy, real joy, in every season. Jesus has truly become your delicious feast, and that kind of joy can only rise from one well: dwelling deeply in the presence of the One whose eyes burn with love.

Dr. Brian and Candice, we want to say a BIG THANK YOU—from the depths of our hearts—for living the message of Psalm 23 with such authenticity, humility, and holy fire, for showing us that union with

Jesus is not only possible but profoundly glorious, and for continually inspiring us to live fully alive, awakened by grace, anchored in love, and set ablaze by the beauty of our King.

We also thank you for your faithful yes to the holy and weighty assignment of The Passion Translation, knowing that Heaven alone understands the full measure of impact your obedience will leave, because what you have stewarded is not merely a translation but an invitation for generations to come, a love song that continues to lead hearts back to the One who restores the soul.

With all honor and our deepest love,

— Ben & Tisha Straup

The Good Shepherd

David's poetic praise to God

"Yahweh is my best friend and my shepherd. I always have more than enough.

He offers a resting place for me in his luxurious love.

His tracks take me to an oasis of peace near the quiet brook of bliss.

That's where he restores and revives my life.

He opens before me the right path and leads me along in his footsteps of righteousness

so that I can bring honor to his name.

Even when your path takes me through the valley of deepest darkness,

fear will never conquer me, for you already have!

Your authority is my strength and my peace.

The comfort of your love takes away my fear.

I'll never be lonely, for you are near.

You become my delicious feast even when my enemies dare to fight.

You anoint me with the fragrance of your Holy Spirit;

you give me all I can drink of you until my cup overflows.

So why would I fear the future?

Only goodness and tender love pursue me all the days of my life.

Then afterward, when my life is through,

I'll return to your glorious presence to be forever with you!"

Psalm 23:1–6 TPT

About the Author

Benjamin Straup is the co-founder and co-leader of Bethesda with his wife, Tisha.

Ben's heart beats with the desire to see people genuinely encounter Jesus Christ without becoming entangled in the wearisome web of religious self-effort.

He has a deep love for sharing the gospel and praying for the individuals God places in his path.

Life is an ongoing journey, and he will be the first to admit he doesn't have it all together — but his anchor is found in the One who holds all things together: Jesus.

Ben loves spending time with his family.

He's a foodie, reptile enthusiast, fly fisherman, and world traveler who laughs often and practices a posture of childlike awe and wonder.

He values authenticity and believes he is at his best when he stays present and playful, keeping the creative flow of divine inspiration wide open.

A Note from the Author

I want to offer a word of transparency and clarity regarding the process behind this book.

I have been told I have ADHD, which I often experience as an overstimulation of data — many streams of thought, insight, and imagination arriving all at once. I frequently know exactly what I want to say; translating those thoughts into linear words, however, can be challenging — an area I am continually growing in. At times, responding to a simple email or message has taken far longer than expected, not because I lack clarity, but because so much information is arriving simultaneously, like a honeycomb of ideas presenting itself all at once.

I also experience patterns consistent with dyslexia. In practical ways, this means I often need to read and reread text to ensure accuracy. Something as small as entering a parking code requires careful attention — checking and rechecking numbers to make sure they have not been transposed or misread. I've learned that slowing down, looking carefully, and absorbing information through repetition allows me to respond with clarity and intention. When I rush, I can miss what I thought I already understood.

These realities have shaped many areas of my life — conversations, teaching, preaching, writing, and daily communication. Yet I do not see them as handicaps. I see them as creative blessings — gifts that carry depth, imagination, and revelation, and that require wisdom and stewardship to be expressed well.

Truth often meets me inwardly — through awe and wonder, imagination, and quiet knowing — long before it becomes words. Learning how to translate that inner landscape for others has been one of my greatest challenges.

God often meets me through Scripture woven into everyday life. Not just a single verse, but a gathering of verses will surface — sometimes echoing one another — while I'm watching a movie, in the middle of a conversation, or sitting with my coffee in the morning. It's as if His Word is responding to the moment, interpreting life as it's happening.

I love to imagine with wonder — to let poetic scenes form in my mind as I sit with Him. Sometimes the insight comes instantly. Other times it unfolds slowly through stillness and attentiveness. As I linger there, I become aware of His nearness and goodness, asking questions, listening, and letting my heart stay open.

In those moments, I feel like a detective searching for hidden treasure. Mystery draws me in. Meaning reveals itself gently. And scenes begin to play out in my imagination — beautiful, layered, alive. This is how God often speaks to me, and it's where my writing is born..

Artificial intelligence has become one of the tools that has helped me steward this gift.

I write the thoughts, the stories, the prayers, and the journey contained in this book. I place the pieces on the table — often all at once — and AI has helped me arrange them into a clear and coherent order so that what lives vividly in my heart can be received clearly by others. In that sense, it has functioned as an editorial assistant or ghostwriter — never replacing my voice, but helping refine and organize it.

Every insight and reflection in this book is my own. AI did not originate the message; it helped me articulate it.

Unexpectedly, this process has also strengthened me. Over time, I have found myself organizing my thoughts more clearly, responding more efficiently, and relying less on assistance than when I began. I cannot fully explain why — but I am grateful for the growth.

This book is not the product of automation. It is the fruit of my own human journey — one marked by wrestling, wonder, patience, and grace — supported by tools that helped bring clarity to what was already alive within.

My hope is that these pages carry the same compassion, depth, and reverence that I feel as I walk with the Shepherd who restores my soul.

— Benjamin Straup

www.ingramcontent.com/pod-product-compliance
Lightning Source LLC
LaVergne TN
LVHW041929070526
838199LV00051BA/2759